NATIONAL MISSING PERSONS HELPLINE 081-392 2000 · Support Youth Rugby · WAVELL WAKEFIELD TRUST TEL: 0902 - 380302 · Be a SPORT

DURAGE · Relocate to Newport, Gwent · CALL-LINE 0891 660 260 · OCS FOR TOTAL BUILDING CARE OCS · CIS PENSIONS · MOWL

Carling's
men

Carling's
men

Mick Cleary

WEIDENFELD & NICOLSON · LONDON

First published in Great Britain in 1995 by
George Weidenfeld & Nicolson Ltd
The Orion Publishing Group
Orion House
5 Upper St Martin's Lane
London WC2H 9EA

ISBN 0 297 83531 9

British Library Cataloguing-in-Publication Data
A catalogue for this book is available
from the British Library.

Designed by Leigh Jones

Litho origination by Pixel Colour Ltd, London

Printed and bound by Butler & Tanner Ltd,
Frome and London

Contents

England's *crowning* moment

In the end it was more a lap of relief than of honour. As Will Carling pushed his way through the throng which had swarmed over the Twickenham turf to acclaim the Grand Slam champions, he cared little about the quality of the match which had just finished. He cared little either for his own personal safety. Choosing to dive into a mob intoxicated not solely on England's success was not perhaps a calm, rational decision. But hang calm, rational decisions. Carling had fulfilled his obligations to those restraints. This moment crowned a magnificent season for England and for Carling in particular. This moment also surely at last banished that irritating ghost of Murrayfield 1990 which had haunted Carling every time a big match loomed, taunting him about his ability to get it right.

On 18 March 1995, England got it right – just. It was a neat irony that the unscheduled lap of honour ended a bit shambolically with Carling getting split from his team-mates and almost bowled over by the spectators swirling all around him. He broke off the celebrations and headed for the sanctuary of the tunnel. The match had followed a similar pattern: good intentions thwarted by meddlesome intruders.

If the performance was a matter of debate, there was no disputing the significance of the result. England had lifted the quadruple of mythical and real trophies – the Grand Slam, Triple Crown, Five Nations championship and the Calcutta Cup. England were Grand Slam champions for the third time in five seasons. England had seen off all challengers. England would head for the World Cup unbeaten. How did it feel, Will? 'Brilliant, just brilliant,' came the breathless reply.

There would be time for more sober assessment in the weeks to come, an opportunity to analyse why it didn't all click and end in a blaze of glory and riot of tries. For now though it was time to savour the beauty of the moment, soak up the applause and the accolades and leave thoughts of hard grounds on the high veldt in

There was a time of course when getting back to work actually meant a return to the daily routine of earning a living. These days the distinction between work and play is blurred. Many of the squad are involved in high-profile, demanding jobs, be it up in the skies with RAF pilot Rory Underwood or buried under a pile of legal documents with solicitor Brian Moore, a commercial litigation partner with Edward Lewis & Co in London. Both men would have been at their posts by 7:30 on Monday morning. (Moore in fact has sometimes had to slip away from the England camp on the eve of a match to tidy up a case awaiting trial.)

Several others have managed to evolve a working relationship with their employer. Work and play time is divided almost equally in these flexible arrangements. By Wednesday morning of an international week, however, everyone is operating under the same system. By midday of the middle of the week all work anxieties are pushed to one side. The focus switches to rugby.

As the chill, snow-flecked rain swept over the England training session at Roehampton on Wednesday, 15 March, the thought of every England player was on the team who stood between them and an historic Grand Slam. For five of the squad there was a slightly uncomfort-

Dwarfing the opposition: Ben Clarke cuts through the Scottish defence.

Nowhere to run: Rob Andrew, tackling Gregor Townsend, and Will Carling stem the Scottish attack.

South Africa for another day. As the evening closed in over the great concrete bowl of Twickenham, the last of the happy revellers disappearing into the shadows, it was time for Carling and his men to indulge in some well-earned, if brief, celebration. Seven months of hard work lay behind them; several weeks of even more intense pressure lay ahead. Time for a drink, old boy, for tomorrow it's back to work.

able feeling of *déjà vu*. Will Carling, Jeremy Guscott, Brian Moore, Rob Andrew and Rory Underwood had travelled to Murrayfield in 1990 in almost identical circumstances. England were heavy favourites, had been playing well and were up against a Scottish side who had struggled to make a mark at all that season yet who had also won all three games up to that point. A Grand Slam, only their second in 33 years, looked a mere formality for England. Formality ended up by slapping them in the face.

It was easy for the rest of the squad to see that painful afternoon as a distant incident. 'It's not even history,' said Victor Ubogu. 'It's ancient history.'

For those who had actually been there – Ubogu couldn't even recall just where he had watched the match – such a perspective was impossible. Sure, times had changed, personnel had changed, even the game had changed. But to reach this stage of rational dismissal involves having to go back and recall the events of the match itself. Once you've done that, how do you get disturbing, nagging thoughts of failure out of your head. Try a little test. For the next five minutes try not to think about a banana. How are you doing? Thought about the banana yet? The mind has a terrible habit of forcing us to contemplate things we'd much rather forget.

This then was the dilemma facing the core of the England squad. It was just not possible to say that Murrayfield 1990 was not on the agenda. Even if they didn't put it there themselves, then someone else would. No, the ghost had to be confronted. And no ordinary ghost was it. Mickey Skinner, flanker that day, confessed that he broke out in a cold sweat for several months afterwards, while Brian Moore's eyes narrow at the mere mention of that fateful afternoon. Carling too was affected by the calamitous defeat, so much so that England under his captaincy the following season retreated into a shell of inhibition, not daring to risk failure again by taking any chances. They won the Grand Slam that year but they won few friends. If the England team of 1991 had stepped onto the psychiatrist's

couch, the men in white coats would still be there now. The memories and the scars ran deep.

'Murrayfield was a big turning point for me

> *A Grand Slam, only their second in 33 years, looked a mere formality for England. Formality ended up by slapping them in the face.*

as captain,' Carling wrote three years later. 'I don't suppose we had considered losing hard enough when it came to the crunch. Now we consider losing in far more depth. When it came it was one hell of a shock. We got it wrong.' 'The dream that was taken away,' is how Carling

When push comes to shove: Victor Ubogu tries to drive forward for England.

9

relived that day in his published diary. 'Maybe we should never have dreamed that way: but we're only human, and I'm sure we all did.'

The dreams this time round were of a more prosaic order: of stifling the Scottish back-row, of imposing a pattern of forward domination, and of then creating opportunities around the field. Or so they all said. You only have to take a look at Carling's face as he skipped around the pitch at the final whistle to appreciate that deep down the hopes were of success if not glory, of silencing troublesome whispers of the past and of embracing history once more. They wanted revenge.

Hard as Carling and the England management tried to make this an ordinary build-up, they failed, if for no other reason than trying to insist that it was just another match and that the Scots were all good chaps and fine players. As the rugby world buzzed with anticipation, as even the man on the Clapham omnibus began to take notice of rugby, and as tickets changed hands for £1,500 a pair on the London black market, it was obvious that this was no ordinary match. A Twickenham seat was the hottest ticket in town. England though worked hard at keeping their feet on the ground. They were well aware that on paper they should win the game comfortably, that if a composite British Lions side were to be picked from the two teams then Scotland would do well to get more than a couple of players included.

Matches though are played on grass, not on paper, as Scotland had proved just a few weeks before in Paris. They had not won in the French capital since 1969 and never at all at the Parc des Princes. This was to be their last chance, for the stadium on the westerly fringes of the capital was to be replaced as the venue of international rugby by a complex being constructed to the north of the city in time for the hosting of the soccer World Cup in 1998. France had just been beaten by England in ignominious fashion at Twickenham and a backlash was expected.

Scotland, for their part, after a run of nine matches without victory, had seen off Canada but had been a shade fortunate to come away with a win against Ireland in their opening Five Nations encounter. Ireland ought to have put the Scots away in the opening 40 minutes at Murrayfield but failed to capitalise on their territorial advantage. But Scotland hung on and

A bloody mouth for one, a bloody nose for the other: Kyran Bracken's cut lip does not prevent him from inflicting a metaphorical grievous blow to Scottish hopes.

fought back through the boot and inspirational leadership of their captain, Gavin Hastings.

And so to Paris. Again Scotland started poorly, were a try down within two minutes and on the ropes. But the halo around the Hastings head was burning brightly that afternoon. Scotland edged their way back, withstood a French counter and finished with a theatrical flourish when Gavin Hastings himself charged dramatically to the line just minutes from the end to seal victory. Wales too were seen off by this deadly combination of Hastings' boot, Hastings' charisma and wonderful support from all those around.

As the England squad checked into the Petersham hotel, a splendid building high up on Richmond Hill in London with views out over the Thames, that Wednesday morning these notes were already firmly pencilled into Jack Rowell's notebook. The England manager was well aware of the threat posed and even if there was little chance of complacency creeping into the England ranks, Rowell wanted to make sure that everyone was aware of just who and what would be lining up against them on the other side of the halfway line in a few days' time. 'The big threat from Scotland is their teamwork,' said Rowell. 'It's how you play as a team that wins a

game of rugby – to have the collective will to win counts for a lot. The Scots have it and they're on the up and up.'

Rowell was also intent on recognising the reality of England's status. The team had been using the services of a sports psychologist, Austin Swain, during the season in an attempt to focus their mental energies. In the old days such preparation would have been dismissed as meaningless mumbo-jumbo and useless in trying to steel hard men in a hard sport. Just before one Scottish team took the field against France, their coach, Jim Telfer, whipped his men into a frenzy, lashing them verbally and physically. One of the players hit back, sending Telfer spinning across the dressing room. As the big man hauled himself to his feet, the rest of team looked on nervously. 'Great,' said Telfer, 'You're ready to play.'

So much for the old-fashioned approach to sports psychology. Rowell, whose mouth has been known to emit the odd barb in its time, may not have any fancy medical letters after his name, but he is a master at the inner game. If it's fine tuning you want, then he is just the man for it. It was blindingly obvious that England were favourites – the bookies had them at 11-2 on with Scotland 7-2 against – and it would do the side no good at all to pretend otherwise.

'Grand Slams are not littered around in rugby history so victory for England has to be an end in itself,' said Rowell. 'That means if people say you are favourites and you feel it's there for good reasons, then why not? Everyone seems to have a huge battle going on to go into games as second favourites but I think that's nonsense. For England it seems that there must be a Dunkirk situation before we do our best but I'd like to think that this England team can go out and

No captain has ever led a country to three Grand Slams as Carling did here.

impose their skills and will on any opposition they meet this year. England have to think big and approach the match that way.'

The days leading up to an international can be a difficult time. For all the stress which may be placed upon getting the machine in working order, of oiling one or two of the rusty elements, there is, in truth, little of real technical or physical purpose which can be achieved in such a short time, particularly once the season is under way. England had already been together for well over a month, with the three-day build-up to each international match, the New Year in Lanzarote and the fortnightly meetings in Marlow in the autumn. What else was there to do? The answer is simple – rest.

Roger Uttley once said that the real benefit of the three-day camp prior to an international was in getting away from the wife and work. It was delivered tongue-in-cheek, but there was more than a jokey half-truth in it. Being able to escape the hassles of home and the office and set the mind on the task ahead is crucial. Victor Ubogu was in self-deprecating mood earlier in the week when he admitted to an interviewer that all he had on his mind was just what the hell

he was going to call his new sports bar due to open shortly in the King's Road, London. 'I can't believe it,' said the England prop. 'I'm supposed to be worrying about beating Scotland on Saturday, not what on earth I'm going to call my bar. What about "Up and Under" perhaps? Oh no, this is getting ridiculous.'

England's routine is well established, although changed in venue this year. The normal meet was at the Stoop Memorial ground in Twickenham on Wednesday. Until recently there used to be just a forwards session, usually on the scrummaging machine. Now the whole squad come together. The work-outs this season have been at the Bank of England ground in Roehampton. The reason for the switch was never made clear, although you don't need a degree in psychology to work out that with former England coach Dick Best at the Stoop, there was a fair chance of there being friction in the air if and when Jack Rowell were to appear. Best's sacking at the start of the 1994-5 season had left a bitter taste in the Harlequin's mouth and even though Rowell claimed the decision was not his but that of the RFU, everyone knew that there was little love lost between the two men.

And so to Roehampton. As the snow showers swirled around and the photographers' cameras clicked, England went through their paces briskly. By now many of the drills are second nature and the task of the coaching staff at this stage is usually to devise either schemes or gimmicks to keep players sharp and on their toes. Here there was no need. Even though this was England's third Grand Slam showdown in five years, failure at this stage would deal a catastrophic blow to their World Cup plan, not to mention grievously wound their own egos. England were very serious and very focussed indeed.

There is a time and place for banter, however, and very necessary it is too if the players aren't to take the field on a Saturday trussed up in a mental straitjacket. At a Courage sponsor's lunch for the players prior to training on Wednesday, Rory Underwood set up Will Carling for a practical joke. In the middle of proceedings a mobile phone bleep was heard coming from Rory's pocket. As he stood to answer the call he pulled a Courage beer can, complete with aerial, from his pocket. 'Hello,' said Rory. 'A message for Will Carling did you say? Yes, I can get it to him.'

The joke unravelled that the captain was due an increase for one of his advertising campaigns, but the bad news was that he would have to eat a year's worth of the product. As jokes go it was hardly in the Oscar Wilde category of sophistication. But as a signal that here was a squad perfectly at ease with itself and each other's company, it was telling. Rory has never been one to thrust himself into the limelight, yet a few weeks earlier he had taken the chair of the team meeting and laid out just what needed to be done.

If England contributed much to their own success by their shrewd planning and whole-hearted endeavour, they were also blessed by the gods. Few sides in any sport can sustain form if blighted by injury. Wales, triumphant just twelve months before, had their faint chance of a repeat performance this time around torpedoed by a savage run of injuries. England had just one injury to contend with in their five months of international rugby, that to Bristol full-back Paul Hull who limped off against Canada in December. His replacement that day was Bath fly-half Mike Catt, who had played few games

at any level in that position.

How did it go? Suffice to say that by the championship's end Catt was being hailed as one of the players of the tournament, his vision, pace, timing and competitiveness marking him down as a sure bet for a long international career. His own preference is for fly-half but such is the threat he poses coming in to the line, that many reckon his future lies in the no. 15 shirt. All England have to do for that to come to pass is to find an adequate substitute for Rob Andrew when he retires!

Fortune favoured England then. They were able to go through the campaign unchanged, only the sixth side ever to do so in the history of the championship. (Of the others, three of them have also gone on to a Grand Slam: France in 1977, Scotland in 1990 and England themselves in 1991.) England's only worry here was a calf strain to reserve hooker Graham Dawe of Bath, an injury which eventually caused the man who had sat on the reserve bench 23 times to withdraw on Friday. With the England A side in South Africa playing against Natal there was a surprise call-up for Saracens hooker Greg Botterman, uncapped and almost unheard of.

No player enjoys the immediate build-up to a match. Far from the stories of folklore, these muscular brutes do not go round banging their heads against dressing-room walls in an effort to

He shall not fall: Tim Rodber symbolises England's firmer resolve on the day as he rebuffs the challenge of Gregor Townsend.

He thought it was all over, and it was: Rory Underwood celebrates victory over the Scots at Twickenham.

psyche themselves up. The need is for calm and control, not emotional cranking-up. The Friday training session was brief, very brief. It was also silent. It was agreed by the squad to have a self-imposed ban on speaking to the press (all apart, that is, from those doing lucrative ghosted newspaper columns, but that's another story). The aim was to avoid any pre-match mud-slinging. It was a reasonable enough excuse even if it did run the risk of drawing attention to the very thing they were trying to avoid. Yes, this was going to be a big, big match, which is why we're acting in this unusual way.

Behind the scenes though the tone was measured and the atmosphere calm. 'Business as usual,' said Victor Ubogu. 'A few words here and there, a chat among the forwards about the importance of tying in their back-row and that was that. Deciding the tactics is the easy bit: it's the waiting that's difficult.'

The supporters have no such problems. The

waiting is very much part of the event. Saturday dawned bright and fair in London and by early morning the skirl of pipes, and lamentous tones of 'Flower of Scotland' could be heard across south-west London. The car parks opened for business at nine o' clock. One other man was also ready for work – Rob Andrew. Far from having his enthusiasm dimmed after so many years of training, the Wasps fly-half, with a record 65 caps to his name, trains and practises harder than ever. He was at Twickenham at 9:15 that morning, grooving his kicking once again. As Rowell commented later that evening after Andrew's record breaking 24 point haul: 'For someone who used to be an "iffy" kicker, Rob was majestic.'

Some kings are born: Andrew has been manufactured, a description which is given as a compliment not as a back-handed criticism. Since he inherited the kicking duties just 12 months before he had left nothing to chance. He had practised and practised and practised. As Gary Player once famously remarked: 'The more I practise, the luckier I get.' As Andrew's second penalty of the afternoon squirted low over the bar, there may have been those who thought the daisy-cutter a fluke. It was nothing of the sort.

But that was for later. As the teams went about their pre-match rituals in their respective hotels a few miles apart, the two sets of supporters went about their pre-match rituals shoulder-to-shoulder in pubs and car parks all around. Scotsmen, many with fake Tam o'shanters and garish, long, ginger wigs à la Russ Abbott, belted out their songs all along the Twickenham approach. In the car parks the plaintive voices of a few poor souls of both persuasions could be heard above the drunken din: 'Anyone got spare tickets for a genuine fan?'

Some chance. The match had been sold out long before the championship began. Now with so much at stake its value had risen to almost unbelievable proportions. Everyone wanted in on the act. Two of the Royal family, Anne, a long-time committed Scottish follower, and brother Edward were in attendance, although they were to be denied the pleasure of presenting the trophy at the end. The West Stand was only partially rebuilt, which meant that the Royal party was seated in the south-east corner. The prospect of getting either the Royals to the other side of the pitch at the final whistle, or the team to them, was too much of a conundrum for the security forces to solve. In theory it was a great shame. In practice, as the stuttering, swamped half-lap of

full-back Mike Catt cope with the bombs raining down on him from the Craig Chalmers howitzer? Gavin Hastings against Rob Andrew kicking for goal? Who could topple the giant Bayfield in the line-out? And, most crucial of all, did the

honour showed, it was probably a wise decision.

As kick-off approached, the essential questions remained the same. How on earth could the Scottish pack cope with the might of the English eight. The Scottish back-row were collectively five years older, five stones lighter and five inches shorter. How would England's tyro

heavy favourites, England, have the mental equipment to cope?

The anthems, the introductions, the whistle. The answers were soon revealed. In all the pre-match hype about what a tumultuous finale this was to the season, there was a distinct, if unspoken, feeling that the whole thing might be one

Work over, time for some rest: The England squad prepare to get stuck into some serious celebrating after clinching their third Grand Slam in five years.

huge let-down. In terms of pure spectacle, it was. In terms of raw excitement, it was too. But in witnessing England keep their nerve, in savouring once more the lion-hearted charges of Gavin Hastings, drawing breath in admiration at the metronomic kicking at goal of Rob Andrew, and, finally, of applauding the fine spirit in which the match was played (the backbiting only came later), there was still something to store away in the memory for fireside nights.

The detail of the match itself will not be recalled in hushed tones in years to come. All the scoring came off the boot: two drop goals from Craig Chalmers and two penalties from Gavin Hastings accounted for the Scottish total, while it was the reassuring sight of Rob Andrew lining up for goal which sustained England supporters throughout the afternoon. Seven times he took aim for goal: only once did he miss. He did though compensate with a towering drop goal from 40 metres in the 64th minute. His second success of the day took him clear of Jon Webb's record aggregate of points for England which stood at 296. By the day's end Andrew had moved level with another milestone, his 24 points equalling the championship record haul set by Frenchman Sebastien Viars against Ireland in 1992.

For those who draw their pleasure from dry statistics, there was ample scope for enjoyment. Gavin Hastings finished with 56 points from the four games, eclipsing his own Scottish championship record set back in 1986. Jason Leonard became England's most capped prop, moving to 39 caps, while Scott Hastings, in his 53rd match, set a similar mark for Scottish centres. No captain has ever led a country to three Grand Slams as Carling did here.

To note also was the injury to Dean Richards who sprung a rib cartilage early in the second half. The sight of the big Leicester man brought to his knees was a first for even the most seasoned observer at Twickenham. England recovered their composure quickly after his departure. Whether Deano would recover in time for the World Cup remained a matter of some concern.

But matches are more than mere numbers on the board. And even if this one lacked colour and verve, there were still moments when the heart beat a little faster and the history book

beckoned. Gavin Hastings was only thwarted by a blend of timing and fortune, when Mike Catt's last-ditch tackle stripped the ball from the grasp of the Scottish captain with the line at his mercy. Tony Underwood went close, so too did Jeremy Guscott. Bayfield was imperious in the line-out, Doddie Weir a constant nuisance and threat for Scotland. Ben Clarke clattered for England from the back-row, Rob Wainwright performed a similar task for Scotland.

In the end then it was the thud on boot which was the dominant feature of the match and on the scoreboard. Who was to blame for this? England hooker Brian Moore had no doubts. No sooner had he finished doing physical battle with the Scots on the field then he was indulging in a bit of verbal jousting. 'I felt sorry for the spectators,' said Moore. 'The Scots ruined the game. They spent the whole game offside, killing the ball or preventing its quick release. At every ruck they were at it – offside, over the top, hands scooping the ball back. You name it, they did it. It was a disgrace and made you want to turn around and kick them. A pity you can't.'

There were many in the England team, and perhaps in the stands, who agreed with Moore. Few though were prepared to voice them publicly. There is no doubt that anyone has the right to his say. However, it seems that there are so many players signed up for ghosted columns (although Moore's initial outburst came on television), that a player is under pressure to deliver some sort of critical perspective, to deliver his pound of flesh. Perhaps the RFU ought to consider gagging the lot. If they do that, then they ought at least to have the decency to compensate the boys for their loss of earnings. What chance

Brought to his knees: A Scottish fan sinks to the Twickenham turf in despair at the final whistle.

is there of that? No chance.

There was certainly little flow to the game. Irish referee Brian Stirling has to shoulder some of the blame for not stamping down harder, but even then he awarded 28 penalties, 19 of them against Scotland. Any more whistles and people would have been asking for their money back.

The taut build-up did not, in the end, produce delirious celebrations. The atmosphere in the England dressing-room was muted, the feeling was one of a job done rather than a glorious sporting triumph achieved. The Scottish response to Moore's outburst was swift and to the point. 'I didn't realise he was the English captain,' said Gavin Hastings tartly. Scottish coach Dougie Morgan was far more scathing. 'I met quite a few of the England lads for the first time this weekend and Will (Carling) and Rob (Andrew) are very nice blokes. At the end of the game you had 29 players shaking hands and congratulating each other and only one man stood out on his own – Brian Moore. He is England's biggest problem and I would not pass the time of day with him.'

The comments, sweet and sour, faded on the night air over Twickenham. Down below, the lorries were moving in to shift the remains of all that

heady stuff which was already contributing to thousands of hangovers. The cranes which towered hauntingly over the partially built West Stand stood silent witness to the work going on down below. By Monday they too would be back in action, financed by part of the record £4 million receipts of Grand Slam day. By the time their own work would be finished, and the new stand completed, the World Cup in South Africa would be over. What state of repair were this England side in? Still under construction or the finished item? Only time would tell.

England were in no doubt what lay before them. The Scots had come close to proving once again that afternoon the truth of that saying about mice and men. Events in South Africa ten months before had shown graphically that it is not just distance which divides the muddy fields of the northern hemisphere from the parched grounds of Africa's southernmost state. For rugby players it's a step into another world, into a rugby culture in which playing styles, surfaces and attitudes to winning are radically different. It took England eight matches to learn that in the summer of 1994. But what an important lesson it was.

Harsh *lessons* on the high veldt

The skies were cloudless, the seas inviting, the surf invigorating, the long, sandy beaches uncrowded. This was early winter in Durban. This was a rugby tour?

Perhaps it was the lotus-land that waved cheerily to the England players every time they opened their hotel room windows which created the slightly unreal air. Or maybe it was the security blanket which was thrown around them on arrival. There they were for all to see, shadowing the England party wherever they went, armed to the teeth, all two of them. Scenes of violence in South Africa, burning tyres, rioting crowds, bull-necked white fascists, had filtered through our television screens in the UK for many months. To see the reality was a shock, and this too might have had an unsettling effect on the team. Streets teeming with people having a good time, blacks and whites; restaurants and bars teeming with young guys and gels anxious to tell you what a great future lay ahead of South Africa. And the two officers assigned to the squad, diligent as they were in their duties, spent a lot of their time humping the tackle bags to training. Just what

the hell was going on? Of course to the north of Durban, high up in the hills of KwaZulu the death toll continued to tick over. Each weekend the tally was announced, the figure of 40 or so deaths accompanied by a sigh of relief that once more it had been a 'quiet weekend in KwaZulu'. This then was the backdrop to England's tour of South Africa.

Putting a rugby tour in a social context is usually a redundant and potentially pretentious exercise. Set of posts, bit of ground, few beers – rugby has a fairly universal, unchanging locale and constituency. And long may it continue. But South Africa was different. This was no ordinary place or time. And even though the England players were cocooned slightly – as all touring parties are – from the everyday realities around them, there was no doubt that they knew, and appreciated, that they were surrounded by momentous events at a momentous time.

And then there was the rugby. England spent a week down at sea-level building up to their first match which was to take place high up on the veldt at Bloemfontein against Orange Free State.

18

They trained ferociously and took care not to indulge themselves on sand, sea or lager. They were fully aware that the countdown to the World Cup had begun and that decent performances here would go a long way to marking the management card in their favour for the real thing in 12 months' time.

So what went wrong? Within five days the tour was off the rails, the midweek and Saturday sides both run ragged by the provincial combinations of Orange Free State and Natal. Ah, but these were strong sides, protested a few. It's well known, they said, that South African provincial rugby was the strongest in the world. (So strong that Queensland had dismantled the same Natal side 21-10 the week before in the final of the Super Ten.) Yes, but it's well known that Australian provincial rugby is the strongest in the world . . .

The apologists for England's poor showing must have known in their heart of hearts that they were clutching at straws. Or perhaps not. Even though England scuffed a victory upcountry against Western Transvaal (24-26), they yet again went down on the second Saturday of the tour, this time by 24-21 to Transvaal. That made it three defeats in four matches, yet afterwards the policy line was that England were improving, that bits of their game were slowly coming together and they remained hopeful. Remained hopeful? This was a team which had put down claimers on the World Cup itself and here they were seemingly accepting defeat to provinces. Many of us in the press box saw it differently. I'd already filed my copy to *The Observer*. The headline read: 'Poor

Where did it all go wrong? Already the surf on Durban beach seems a distant memory for the England captain as the realisation of defeat by 21–6 against Natal begins to sink in.

(opposite) Bloodied, beaten but not bowed: A groggy Rob Andrew, helped from the field at the end of the Natal match by Ben Clarke and Martin Johnson, was to enjoy his moment of revenge a fortnight later in the first Test.

Deluded England' Part of the match report beneath it included these indicting paragraphs:

'The English game must now be held to account. It seems trapped in a prison of inhibition, with players never daring to probe adventurously or to try and conjure something from nothing. The whole ethos is flawed and glaringly revealed as so in this country. England have deluded themselves so far on this tour that they are being hammered by referees and so prevented from imposing themselves on their opponents. They are seeking false solace in such thoughts. Their sense of injustice allows them to hide from the painful truth; that they are a wooden, one dimensional truth.

'They insist that the percentage game pays dividends. It may do so on the muddy fields of Europe but here it is exposed as a limited strategy. The tour management now have a huge task on their hands just six days before the first Test. They must be brave and abandon their pre-tour ideas.'

What happened six days later? England stuck to their plans and knocked South Africa from here to eternity. (And they got to meet Nelson Mandela.) They were 20 points up within a quarter of an hour, well on their way to recording what was one of their finest ever victories in international rugby. So, the sensation-seeking, cynical, unseeing, unknowing hacks got it wrong again, eh?

If it hadn't been for a snatched conversation in a hotel lift a week earlier, then I might well have felt a tad uncomfortable after that first Test. However, coming back from the Transvaal game I bumped into Les Cusworth in the hotel. I knew

Where is the cavalry? Tony Underwood hangs on grimly when swamped by the Transvaal defence, hoping that Dean Richards will soon help him out.

what I'd just written and I'd heard what the management had said at the press conference. 'Satisfied with that then, Les?' 'I could cry,' said Cusworth, one of the nicest as well as one of the astutest men in rugby. 'Inside, when you watch that sort of rugby, your heart weeps.' A few words which spoke volumes.

The reasoning behind England's transformation this past season, from a team with near and inadequate horizons to one with more expansive vistas, playing a more considered and more appropriate game, was captured in Cusworth's mood and comment. England were going nowhere. He knew it. So too did Jack Rowell, even if for the sake of morale, they were not going to say it on the record.

The first Test was won on character and conviction, assets which should never be downplayed and ones which England have in abundance. Of course there was some rugby in there too. But it was not until their return to England that the squad and the coaches began to put into practice the lessons learnt from the tour. And the man who lead the way was Jack Rowell.

If England were battling to come to terms with alien conditions, styles of play, altitude and embarrassing defeat, they were also to have to come to terms with a new manager. In retrospect it was small wonder that England under-performed on this tour. Things were changing all around them – be it the laws of the game, the pecking order in world rugby with South Africa now back in the frame, or the man who picked the side.

As a race the English are not comfortable with change. Convention, tradition, procedure – these are the touchstones of its history. Reliability, loyalty, consistency – these are the

Taking the hiss: As if they weren't already suffering enough on the rugby field, Rory Underwood and Victor Ubogu subject themselves to ordeal by snake.

(opposite, bottom left) Do I not like what I see? The England bench show their emotions as coaches Dick Best (gaping with horror) and Les Cusworth (simply glum) take in the ordeal of the Transvaal match.

virtues most admired. That is not to say that there is no place for the maverick: just that the maverick has to fight a little bit harder to make his mark. That is not to say either that innovation and imagination are not cherished and appreciated. They are, as the literary and cultural history of the country shows. But it takes time. Jack Rowell saw that, and he took his time.

The sudden resignation of manager Geoff Cooke a few months before had come as a huge shock to everyone involved in the England set-up. (It probably came as a shock to Cooke himself that he finally summoned up the nerve to actually go through with it all.) Cooke had been in the post for over six years, a stewardship which saw England move from under-achievers to achievers. Two Grand Slams were notched up and one missed. Anyway, Cooke looked set for the World Cup. He said it, his contract (albeit tacit) said it, and his long-time captain, Will Carling, said it. Then, one Monday morning, just five days before England were due to take on France at the Parc des Princes, came the shock news that he had resigned.

He couldn't have done. He must have been pushed. Those stuffed suits in the RFU, who had always frowned at Cooke's close relationship with the players, must have finally put the knife in. Conspiracy theories swirled all around. And they were all wrong. Cooke had had enough. Enough of the motorway, enough of endless meetings and enough of being a manager rather than a hands-on coach.

'I had more or less made up my mind to go before last Christmas,' explained Cooke, 'when it became obvious to me that it was time to finish. I was getting weary of living in a goldfish bowl.

A mountain to climb: Mike Catt and Jason Leonard on top of Table Mountain, Cape Town, taking stock of all that South Africa has to offer.

I thought it would be a bit selfish to go after the New Zealand game and I believed that once the championship started I would rediscover my enthusiasm. It hasn't really happened and I realised I didn't want to go to South Africa in the summer in my present role as manager, standing watching interminable practice sessions. I'm tired. I need a break and I think it's in the best interests of the team. A new man will bring a fresh perspective, fresh ideas.'

And so he did. Jack Rowell's appointment was not actually a formality, although it ought to have been. He was the only man for the job. The RFU, bless 'em, have been known to have had a few problems in the past in spotting the blindingly obvious. This time their eyesight was perfect.

Rowell's impact will be considered in more depth in the next chapter. For the time being the significance of his arrival may be confined to one

thing – the end of the road for Dick Best. The England coach knew from the moment that the news broke of Cooke's resignation that his days were numbered. Why the hell someone didn't have the decency to officially tell him so is no mystery – insensitive cackhandedness is a trait of most governing bodies – but why they prolonged it is.

Jack Rowell is no man in a suit. He spends enough time in that role in the real world. So even though he was brought in to replace Geoff Cooke, who was a touchline manager, there was simply no doubt that Rowell would want to have a hands-on involvement with the team. Perhaps he was buying himself time or perhaps he was giving this squad a little rope with which to hang itself. If they flunked in South Africa, then Rowell could wade in and do things his way. There are many convoluted theories as to why Dick Best was put through the unnecessary embarrassment, humiliation even, of the South African tour. Rowell never allowed himself to get close to Best at all on the tour knowing that things would change come September.

The politics of it all are for Best and Rowell to sort out. Cooke's words on departure, that the team needed a fresh impetus, were, in hindsight, right on the button. Best, who had come to the job after the last World Cup, had built his reputation at Harlequins. His sides there, in their early days certainly, were renowned for their adventure and invention. Strangely and sadly, his England teams never achieved that consistency of style. But let it be said too that a Grand Slam was won, in 1992, and wonderful victories over New Zealand and South Africa (twice) recorded.

But early in 1994 he admitted to me that his once sacrosanct devotion to style and grace on a rugby field had been superseded by a realisation that, at international level, winning was everything. Was he happy about this? 'I was devastated,' he said.

The romantic turned pragmatist. It didn't suit Best and it didn't suit England. Videos, charts, statistic sheets may all have endorsed his case that this was the only route to World Cup success, one which it was said that the Australians were marching along. The narrowness of the vision was exposed in South Africa.

Theories are all very grand and all very meaningful on paper. But just because they sound good does not mean that anyone believes that they will work. The thoughts of Rowell and Cusworth (whom Rowell brought in as assistant coach) were as yet no more than gentle whispers in the background. Maybe some of the players were already in tune with their way of thinking. But no matter how well you expound an idea, there is nothing like seeing the evidence of it before your very eyes to turn nodding approval into firm conviction. In South Africa, wherever England went, they saw the evidence with their own eyes. This lot were playing a different game entirely.

The early hiccups on the tour – defeats by Orange Free State (22-11) and Natal (21-6) – could have been explained away by the difficulty of acclimatisation, by the fact that the first and second strings had been mixed. It was all nonsense. England were off the pace. The standard and style of play in the warm-up matches, whether played between U-21 provincial sides or reserve teams, was way ahead of that seen on any ground in England.

The parched surfaces of course meant that the handling and running game was much easier to bring off. But it was the attitude of these players, their willingness to probe for openings and to test defences, which most impressed. When South Africa were re-admitted to the international fold three years ago their rugby was wooden, stilted and lumpy. They were old men out of step with the modern idiom. So it was not just a case of the hard grounds inevitably producing a vibrant brand of rugby. In those few years the South Africans had taken a long, hard look at what might be needed to get back to where they felt they rightly belonged. That is,

Getting stuck in at last: For almost the first time on the tour England take the game by the scruff of the neck, which led to several flare-ups in this match in Kimberley against South Africa A.

not just up with the world leaders, but to become the world leader. Sometimes, just sometimes, you have to admire their arrogance. And so this more positive, more all-embracing brand of rugby evolved.

England saw it and, slowly, liked what they saw. It's very difficult within the close confines of a touring party, where commitment to the common cause is everything, to step back and see the broader perspective. That is probably why Rowell preferred to detach himself from the day-to-day running of the tour. A few players in the squad though were not too taken either with the emphasis being placed on route one rugby – kick long and wait for the opposition to make mistakes.

It was the morning of the England A match in Kimberley which not only turned the tour round but which perhaps also set England along their way to this season's style of play and accompanying success. Three of the senior players that day – Wasps captain Dean Ryan, scrum-

half Steve Bates and Bath fly-half Stuart Barnes – got together after breakfast and thrashed out just what they were going to do. They'd had enough of sitting back and crossing fingers. 'Let's give it a lash,' said Barnes.

And give it a lash they did. For the first time on tour there were South Africans on the back foot, defending frantically as England mixed the game up, running from certain positions, kicking from others. It's true the game was lost, 19-16, but the whole mood of the squad was different that night. The second string had shown what was possible. (Mind you, Rowell did quite rightly put a dampener on this quasi-euphoric state by reminding some of the players that they had actually lost the game.)

Looking back it may be a touch fanciful to attribute England's game this season to a few words between the boys on the plane to Kimberley. Little moments though do linger, particularly in sport. Mood is an intrinsic part of performance. The squad were in desperate need

Proving them all wrong: Rob Andrew gathers his own kick ahead to score the try which helped send England on the way to a stunning victory in the first Test in Pretoria.

of a boost, no matter how threadbare and transient. England A gave it to them that afternoon. Three days later England took South Africa apart in front of the masses packed into Loftus Versfeld in Pretoria. What a time for Nelson Mandela to choose to watch his first test match in decades.

The South African tour, then, was a watershed. It marked the final point of the Cooke-Best era and the beginning of the Rowell regime. England had the best of all tours in many ways. The memory of that dramatic afternoon in Pretoria will fuel their confidence for many years to come, no matter the collapse to defeat seven days later in the second Test in Cape Town. Every side needs a little hope and England certainly got that from the first Test. But every aspiring side needs sudden shocks to the system, sharp reminders of their limitations and mortality. England, in losing three of the eight games, certainly got that. The route to the top is never easy and if suffering is any sort of prerequisite to success, then England may well be destined for ultimate honours on their return to South Africa this summer. In South Africa they hurt badly. Jack Rowell was not slow to take advantage of that pain.

Hopes in tatters: Brian Moore's ripped shirt was evidence of the furious riposte from the Springboks in the second Test at Newlands.

the Management

Many expected a cliché: what they got was a man full of subtlety, complexity, vision, determination, warmth, passion, soul, intellect – the list goes on. Just when you might think that you've got Jack Rowell figured out and are about to put him into his pigeon-hole along comes another unexpected tilt of behaviour and character and you're left floundering for an explanation. Suffice to say that he is simply his own man with his own ways. And very successful they are too.

When Geoff Cooke resigned, there was only one man in the frame. Would he get the job, however? Cooke too was a man who made his mark in a singular way. There were many behind the scenes at the RFU who disliked his frequent place in the headlines, his progressive views on amateurism and other related topics, his high profile, his great honesty and his refusal to duck issues. Time for a change perhaps? Back to someone whose strings we can can tug from Twickenham, someone who will issue the platitudes we want, knot his tie properly, project the RFU image and simply do as he's told.

Ten years ago it's conceivable that Rowell would have been passed over for someone who was a bit closer to the party line. In fact Rowell had been passed over. It's not as if he had suddenly shot into the limelight in the nineties, unheralded and unknown. He had been at Bath since the mid-seventies, turning what was a small, homespun, very unproductive club, who were very much the poor relations of those two other West country outfits Bristol and Gloucester into probably the most consistently successful club in the whole of world rugby. He coached Gosforth to the John Player Cup win in 1976 before he headed south. Under his guidance Bath won the league seven times and the Cup four times. Just a couple of months after he acceded to the England post the club won the double for the second time in three years. Yes, but apart from all that, just what has he done?

In the day job he was executive director of Dalgety plc, a £1 billion food and agriculture combine based in Market Harborough. Twice a

30

week Rowell would head back to Bath for the 300 mile trip to training. He was responsible for four companies and 4,000 employees. For this work (which he has now cut back on) Rowell received, in all probability, a six figure salary. For his rugby work he receives nothing. Sounds like the RFU got a good deal. His schedule would bring most of us to out knees. Rowell thrives on it. 'I need to be active,' he says. 'Travelling time is thinking time.'

For all his success at Bath it was not until 1992 that Rowell was brought into the England fold, as coach to the England B side. Why the wait? The RFU were guarded, wary of Rowell's hands-on, all-embracing ways. Twickenham wanted to control the direction of the game, not have it controlled for them. Rowell was also so fiercely loyal to Bath that there had occasionally been spats between the club and the RFU as to whose interests should have priority at any given time. 'It may be good enough for England, but it's not good enough for Bath,' Rowell used to say, only half tongue-in-cheek, to his legion of returning international players at the next club

An early challenge: Tim Rodber's dismissal in the brutal match against Eastern Province thrust Rowell into the spotlight when the disciplinary panel, of which he was a part, deemed that sending-off was to be punishment enough for the backrow forward.

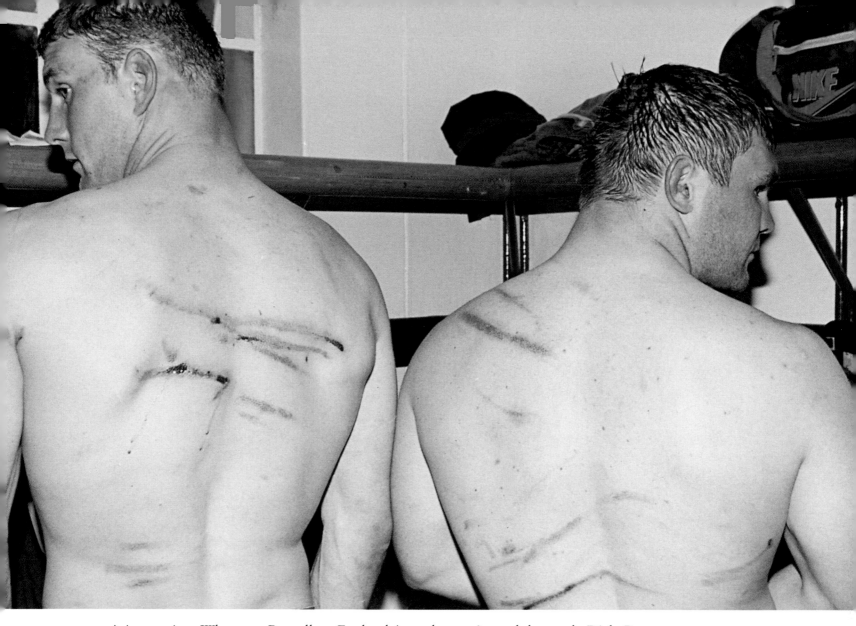

training session. Whatever, Rowell, as England A manager, was now very much part of the set-up. Now was to be his time.

If his appointment was greeted with widespread acclaim in the media, there must have been shivers down the backs of a few England players on hearing the news. Chief among them might well have been Will Carling.

Bath was not so much a rugby club, more a family, one in which the virtues of loyalty, commitment, belief in the cause and shared responsibility were etched in stone. If you joined the family, you swore allegiance to its ways. Such kinship bred an inner toughness in all its players and is, above all other reasons, just why Bath have dominated the game for so long. At Carling's club, Harlequins, there were many times when the club failed to put out the same side two weeks running, particularly in the chill depths of winter. 'All very valid reasons for

absence,' as club coach Dick Best was apt to comment. 'Good snow at Val d'Isere or sales at Harrods.'

Carling too had often explained that England was his club; that, as captain, his prime obligation was to his country. Over many seasons Carling averaged no more than about fifteen top-line matches for Harlequins. Jack Rowell and Will Carling? It hardly seemed as if it would be a meeting of like minds.

As seen earlier, what you expect Rowell to do is not always the way it happens. Carling is captain now through to at least the end of the World Cup and has had his best international season for three years. Just what is it that Rowell has that makes people tick?

If you listen in some unknowing quarters, they'll tell you that Rowell is a big man with a big voice, one who lays down the law and expects others to follow. There's nothing wrong

Violent ways of violent men: The scars on the face of Jon Callard and on the backs of the England forwards Lawrence Dallaglio and John Mallett show what prompted Rowell's defence of Rodber.

with such an approach of course - but it's not Rowell's. It's easy to make an impression by being a hectoring, dogmatic, loud-mouthed, bullying type. Making an impact, and a lasting one, is nigh on impossible with such tactics. Rowell uses whatever means are appropriate. If someone needs a bollocking that is what they get. If an arm round the shoulder and a few soothing words is what is called for, then out comes the arm and down goes the voice. Rowell relates to people and to situations as he sees fit. He may demand success but he is no blinkered taskmaster.

'That's an image of yesteryear,' says Rowell. 'It's a caricature and out of sync with reality. I have to deal successfully with people for a living and there's no way that you would get the best from them if they were trembling before you every time you opened your mouth. I'm not into blasting people just for the sake of it. Now and then harsh words are appropriate. You must always be wary of easy images. Just because Victor Ubogu smiles a lot doesn't mean that he doesn't take his rugby seriously. People are structured differently and you have to take account of that.'

Victor Ubogu endorses what Rowell says. 'A lot of people get me wrong,' says the Bath and England prop. 'They see my laid-back exterior and jump to a snap conclusion. Jack is the only one who's got me worked out, the only coach I've ever come across who knows how to get the best from me.'

When former England full-back Jon Webb arrived at the Recreation Ground in Bath, so disenchanted with the game that he had left Bristol and come to Bath just for one last roll of the dice, Rowell wasted no time in telling him what was wrong with his game. 'I didn't actually like what he said about me,' recalls Webb. 'But that was not the point. His comments were actually about me and that was just what I needed at the time – someone to show an interest in me.'

Tough as old boots, soft as a doting auntie – Rowell can swing both ways. Man management is his great strength. The nuts and bolts of coaching, the minutiae of technical adjustment, are not for him. Certainly there was no way he would have come to the England job and accepted a brief of pressing flesh at post-match dinners and making ceremonial speeches. 'The administrative side of the manager's job is horrific,' says Rowell. 'There was no satisfaction in it for me. Being pushed up into that role with England A was a disappointment for me. You're removed from the inner sanctum.'

Rowell wanted direct involvement even though in Dick Best there was a man already there in a tracksuit. So although Rowell was officially appointed as manager there was no way that he would remain on the touchline and simply get on with organising the team bus and other such fulfilling duties. 'I think we can learn from soccer,' said Rowell, shortly after he took up the reins. 'The manager there often has a team of coaches under him. His role is to set the pattern.

*(opposite)
To kick or to run? There was no question in the old days when England opted for the aerial route. Rowell set about broadening their horizons.*

The gentle touch: Rowell was quick to bring in Les Cusworth to lend his experience and benign ways to the cause.

That is what I will do. It's this broad strategy that England have lacked over the last couple of seasons.'

In private Rowell had very definite views as to where he thought England were going wrong. In public though he spoke only of the need for evolution not revolution. Again he did not wish to be branded in simplistic terms, as the man who was coming in with an axe over his shoulder bent on wreaking havoc to get his own way. Rowell knew also that it is never simply a case of telling someone what to do. Self-discovery is always a more substantial and lasting state of awareness than mere discovery. The trick is to create the conditions by which someone can work it all out for themselves. The end may

appear the same: the means are very different. And it is the means which, in the final analysis, lays down the deeper roots and so yields the greater fruit.

'If things are a shambles you can apply management directives,' says Rowell. 'But if things are going well you invert the pyramid and have the workers, in this case the players, at the top. It is as simple and as complex as that. If you are going into a team where some of them have been around for 50 caps, you have to take the players along with you.'

And what great truths were unearthed by the players on this voyage of discovery? Fairly elementary ones, to be honest. It was obvious, particularly to the poor mug who'd paid hundreds of

pounds for a black market ticket that season, that England were not scoring enough tries. And yet, much as the critics panned England for their shortcomings near that elusive white try line, counsel for the defence would always insist that it did not matter how the points were scored, as long as more of them were scored than by the opposition. It was a view which did not find much favour with Rowell. 'England have lost the knack of scoring tries,' said Rowell. 'We will have to explore more options. There's no point leaving Rory Underwood in the cold. Tries are important. I don't know how you can expect to consistently win games without scoring them.'

The statistics for England's five matches of the 1993-4 season back up to what Rowell said: four were devoid of tries and the fifth, against Wales, brought two - one from a line-out on the Welsh line. This season, with admittedly two gentle looseners against Romania and Canada, they have scored 23 tries. 'Before we went to South Africa I told them that two tries per season wasn't good enough,' said Rowell.

Again it was the evidence of their own eyes, usually peering backwards at a disappearing South Africa backside on its way to the tryline, which convinced the players. The talk began to focus on the need to evolve a more complex game. 'The modern game demands it, 'said Rowell. Forwards have to be brought in in a more positive fashion. They have to develop a more rhythmic pattern. Integration between backs and forwards is crucial if we are to play from anywhere. It's got nothing to do with providing entertainment. Simply that it gives you more options and therefore more opportunities to score points and so win.'

Rowell knew, and said so on many occasions, that England would never win the World Cup unless that managed to become more sophisticated. Now, there had long been in the English game, a fly-half – the essential playmaker of any side – who met many, if not, all Rowell's requirements. He was also in tune with the Rowell ethos of winning at all times and in all situations. Accepting defeat was simply not part of the creed. He was talented, forthright, challenging, colourful, all things that Rowell held dear. And he played for Bath.

'Stuart Barnes is a one-off,' Rowell once said. 'He has an on-board computer in his head which clicks through all the options open to him.

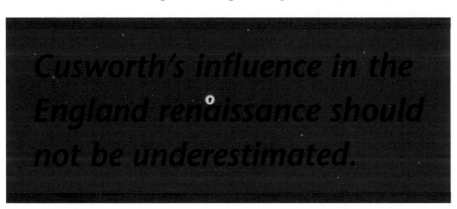

Cusworth's influence in the England renaissance should not be underestimated.

He knows where he is all the time. He's the equivalent of the American quarter-back, and it needs a very special man to be able to do all that. Stuart Barnes is a maestro.'

Quite what might have developed between Rowell and Barnes in the England set-up, we shall never know. At the end of the South African tour, when injury robbed Barnes of a specific opportunity to have a real shot at edging Rob Andrew out of favour, Barnes announced that he was retiring.

The marriage was not to be. There is no guarantee, of course, that Jack Rowell would have favoured his one-time Bath captain over Rob Andrew. That would perhaps have been too predictable. Barnes though was undoubtedly in line with Rowell's thinking on threequarter play, one which, it must be said, Andrew has taken on board magnificently. More of that anon.

The presence of Barnes in the ranks has always been a spur to Andrew to keep on top of his game. Barnes's retirement though did not mean that it was time to switch off, to take a breather after so many years of intense rivalry. With Rowell around, you see, there is no such thing as a comfort zone. 'Perhaps everything was a bit cosy,' said Andrew. 'We all need a change of stimulus from time to time, and I certainly felt challenged when Jack came in.'

Small wonder that Rowell never plays down his image too much. If the myth alone is enough to galvanise people into action, then why bother to modify it. It doesn't even matter what Rowell is actually like. It's what people think he's like that's important.

Rowell, then, deliberately took a back seat in South Africa. He had brought in Les Cusworth, but still it was Best who called most of the shots during the tour. With Best gone, Cusworth assumed a key position in the set-up and was very much on the same wavelength as Rowell, whom he had worked alongside with England A. If Rowell wanted England to attack the gain line more often, then Cusworth was the man to help them do it.

There was always a charm and grace about Les Cusworth during his playing days at Leicester. He won only 12 caps for England, an under-achievement which was largely the result of bone-headed management and selection which instructed the essentially running fly-half to kick who, when orders were obeyed, was promptly dropped.

As with Rowell, Cusworth too is also portrayed in a somewhat inappropriate, one-dimensional way. In short, as a romantic, carefree soul intent only on pleasing the crowd and weaving beautiful patterns across a rugby field. Such an image is a long, long way from the truth. Cusworth may be a genial, kindly soul, and he did, it's true, often thrill with his scampering runs. But, above all else, like Rowell, he believes in winning. He is a Yorkshireman after all.

Cusworth's influence in the England renaissance should not be underestimated. Rowell may well apply the broad brush to the canvas but if

All we are saying is give him the ball: Jack Rowell stated very early in his tenure that England had to involve Rory Underwood more in the action.

the detail is not right then the product will look a mess. Cusworth not only has the ideas he has the credibility. The players believed in him because of who he was and what he had done. Even if he did start talking to them about that funny 13-a-side game they play up north.

'I watch a lot of rugby league,' Cusworth reveals. 'They're not just great with the ball in hand, particularly the Australians, but they run such sharp, intelligent angles. When the Kangaroos toured here last autumn I went to several of their sessions to pick up ideas.

'Our game had become stagnant. I sometimes used to wonder what on earth I was doing watching games. It was like watching paint dry. Kicking seemed to be the only real option considered. In the southern hemisphere a player will always take a look before they kick. Here our lads would kick and then take a look. It was simply a question of awareness because our boys have the talent. They just weren't using it.

'The southern hemisphere have had a head start on us in many ways in their preparations because of their ready acceptance of what the revised laws permit. Here we were slow to appreciate the possibilities. I think some of our senior clubs lacked ambition. The game was getting slower and slower, the maul was being overdone and there were limitations across the board.

'That is why in South Africa, in the first fortnight of the tour in particular, England caught a cold.'

In a neat reversal of the facts of the calendar one of the major tasks which lay before the new boys, Rowell and Cusworth, was how to persuade the old hands, Carling, Moore, Andrew and Rory Underwood, to come into their corner. In the end not much persuasion was needed. The players were working it out for themselves.

Even so the relationship between the old and the new, between management and senior players, was of crucial importance. If Rowell got it wrong, or even chose to drop some of them, then the whole harmony and stability of the England squad could have been in jeopardy. Whichever way you looked at it, the veteran quartet of players, were key figures.

Will Carling

The season's end
and still in
charge: All Will
Carling's anxieties
about a change
in captaincy
under the new
regime quickly
evaporated.

The headlines screamed out across the front page of the *Telegraph* sport supplement. For most people it made riveting reading. If you were Will Carling, it also made very painful reading indeed.

Stuart Barnes, who had been a team-mate just a few months before on England's summer tour to South Africa, was putting the boot in with all the force of an 18 stone lock forward charging through a ruck. Carling, he thought, was flat, stale, uninterested and lacking in any sort of commitment to his club, Harlequins. A few of us might have raised one or two of the charges in the occasional match report from the Stoop but in more muted tones and in a less prominent position. Maybe it was a quiet Sunday on the *Daily Telegraph* sports desk. Maybe the boys knew a good story when they saw it. They certainly gave it the sort of treatment of which any tabloid would be proud. They went for it in a big way. This was a public indictment of the highest order.

And how has it affected Will Carling? Brought him to his knees? Left him a quivering neurotic mess, just one tantrum away from a straitjacket. Er, not exactly. Will Carling has just had his best international season for at least three years. In fact some pundits would say he's played the best rugby of his life. Stuart Barnes, what did you do to this man?

There was far more behind Carling's rejuvenated play, and the smile on his face throughout the season, than a few barbed verbal bombs from Stuart Barnes. In fact there's far more to Will Carling than superficially meets the eye. He may appear self-confident and aloof, to be existing on a plane way above the great unwashed. In truth he's a sensitive soul, prone to the same sort of anxieties and doubts which swirl round all of us at one time or another. And he's not the only one.

What is remarkable about this current England squad is just how well the old (in terms of experience) campaigners have performed. Will Carling, Rob Andrew, Brian Moore and Rory Underwood (you can even include Jerry Guscott and Dean Richards in this category) have all been through some tough times together. You would be unchallenged by anybody if you said that two

of them – Carling and Andrew – are in the best form of their lives. How ironic it is that it is these two players who have drawn the most criticism down the years as well. And no matter what any player may tell you, they do read the newspapers and the adverse press does sting . . .

'You can't get away with ignoring it,' says Carling. 'Even if you don't read it yourself then some so-called mate will ring to tell you what's been written. You can't pretend that it doesn't hurt either. It certainly hurts me. As for Stuart Barnes, I took exception to him questioning my attitude. How does he know? It's fair enough to say that my tackling was weak, or passing poor, but not that my body language told him some-

thing. Is he a psychiatrist or what? It was a totally subjective piece and poor journalism. Criticism in general is legitimate even if none of us likes it.'

The secret, according to former England cricket captain Mike Brearley, is to reply to critical attacks with your intellect not your ego. Carling replied with his feet. Suddenly they began to move again. And with his hands. Suddenly they were feinting and handing off again. And with his body. Suddenly Will Carling looked a big man on a rugby field again, full of menace and authority. He actually looked as if he were enjoying himself again. And such a look had not been seen for quite a few years.

It may appear all swank and glamour being

The way it was: Former England manager Geoff Cooke, whose resignation stunned everyone in the game, enjoys a joke with the man he made one of the youngest ever England captains in 1988.

England captain, and certainly Carling would not think to moan about his lot. But in the past four years he has had a fairly stormy ride through the waters of international rugby. On the field he had struggled to hit that groove of attacking sharpness which was such an important and engaging part of his play in the early years. Off the field he had spats with the rugby union, some of whom thought he was too big for his boots and coining too much money from the

An early sighting of the rejuvenated Carling came in the autumn match against Romania which England won, 54–3.

45

game. He fell foul of divisional selectors when he missed a London training session. There was friction with one or two of the England players as to the division of spoils from the commercial activities. Things got so bad at one point in the early nineties that Carling phoned Rob Andrew and told him that he wanted to give up the

(well almost) he seethed and sulked, struggling to come to terms with this massive blow to his ego. He saw it as public humiliation and a sign that perhaps the end was near. Rather than take part in a Sunday training session with the second string who were preparing for a tough last game of the tour against Waikato, Carling took to his

England captaincy. He came through that one.

And then came the Lions tour to New Zealand in the summer of 1993. For the first time in his career Carling was dropped. How did he react? Take it on the chin and say 'Well done, old bean,' to his replacement, Scott Gibbs. In public this is, of course, what he did. In private

hotel room. To all intents and purposes he was off the tour, on the point of packing his bags and heading for the first plane home. To the surprise of everyone, including the tour management of Geoff Cooke, Ian McGeechan and Dick Best, he turned full circle and went out and played his finest game of the tour. As nearly everyone else in

When English eyes are smiling: Tony Underwood races up to support his captain in the opening Five Nations match against Ireland.

that dirt-trackers side fell lamely and limply by the wayside, Carling stood firm. (So too did Stuart Barnes – funny old game, sport, and the company you find yourself in.)

It had been a bad tour though for Carling. The 1993-4 season was also one of occasional peaks and some disturbing troughs. The All Blacks were seen off in splendid style but the championship campaign faltered. A snatched, scuffed win at Murrayfield was followed by defeat at home to Ireland, Carling's first loss as captain at Twickenham. 'There were times when I was not in control out there,' he admitted afterwards.

Geoff Cooke resigned, the team bounced back brilliantly to see off the French in Paris and the championship finished in some style for England with convincing victory over Wales. And then came South Africa.

No one really knew how Will Carling would deal with this past season. If you were a betting man you had to lean towards some attractive odds that he might lose both the captaincy and his place. Jack Rowell was reckoned not to fancy Carling's hot and cold moods and might also favour Bath centre Phil de Glanville once Jerry Guscott was restored to full working order. So ran the conspiracy theory anyway. What was it then that turned Carling back into a raging tornado in a white shirt?

Jack Rowell's famed man-management skills obviously had a large part to play. But so too did Will Carling himself. It's no coincidence that both his home life and his business career stabilised in the last twelve months. His marriage to Julia Smith, a former girlfriend of rock guitarist Jeff Beck, seems to have brought him security and contentment. Although if part of Will yearned for a quieter, more private domestic life, he was unlikely to get it with Julia. 'Right Said Fred' and sundry other celebs were guests at the lavish wedding reception last summer at Castle Ashby in Northamptonshire. Early in the New Year Mrs Carling did a two week fill-in stint as presenter of Channel 4's Big Breakfast and she also features alongside her husband in a TV commercial.

His business too has enjoyed a profitable year. Carling set up his company, Insights, four years ago to give motivational seminars to cor-

Flattering to deceive: The bright lights and sharp suits are not always the preferred backdrop for the naturally shy Carling.

porate groups. Carling was accused by the likes of former England prop Jeff Probyn of trading on his name, a name created on the back of old sweats like Probyn. Of course Carling was trading on his own name and position. He'd have been a fool not to, as even Probyn admits. There was more to it than that, however. No business man in his right mind (although this quality is not always readily apparent in the City) would fork out a few thousand of his firm's money just to listen to some claptrap about winning Grand Slams. He could quite easily go to a rugby dinner and, for a fraction of the price, get that.

No, after the initial novelty wore off, Carling had to put a proper business together. Using the services of several top sportsmen – Mike Brearley, Adrian Moorehouse and Gary Lineker – Carling created a successful package which appeals and which works. The company

returned decent profits on trading last year. 'The business has become more and more successful,' says Carling's agent, Jon Holmes, the man who also looks after the likes of Gary Lineker and David Gower. 'It's become less and less dependent for its success on Will's profile on a rugby pitch. He's proved that he can survive and even thrive in a proper business environment. The whole thing has given him a sense of permanence which perhaps he didn't have before.'

Will's feelgood factor was enhanced almost immediately by Rowell's announcement that he was to be captain for the season. In Geoff Cooke's era, this was a routine appointment. Carling rejects the notion that he and Cooke were too close, that their long-standing relationship created a comfort zone which was partially responsible for the fires dimming in the captain and so leading him to under-perform. 'I know full well that Geoff would have dropped me if he felt it had been in the team's interests,' said Carling. 'I could not have respected him if that had not been the case. We were very close but the line between player and selector was never crossed. I might be in on selection meetings but it was always a relief to be in the team.'

Under Cooke though there was no doubt that Carling was an automatic choice. There is no doubt either that the way the team operated, the procedures, the style, the approach, were very much the product of the Cooke-Carling think tank. And why not? The pair of them, in their different ways, had turned English rugby around, imposing a structure and sense of order on the whole set-up where none had existed before. Carling was the focal point of all that went on.

Rowell, however, changed all that. Not in any overt way by formally downgrading Carling's responsibilities. Rowell works far more subtlely than that. He realised that Carling would thrive if the pressure were taken off him. But to publicly demote Carling in the name of delegation would be to run the risk of alienating him, of even humiliating him. Gradually though Rowell began to involve more and more of the players in the decision-making process, getting them to work together as a team rather than as a captain and 14 others. The old guard of Brian Moore, Rob Andrew and Dean Richards were

In the eye of the storm: Carling prepares his men to withstand a second half fight-back by the Springboks in the first Test.

49

central to this strategy.

'Jack is a complex character who keeps us all on our toes,' says Andrew. 'As he has grown into his job, so he has taken the pressure off Will. He drives us hard to think about what we are doing. He has given Will a new lease of life.'

Dean Richards is a man of big actions but few words. When he does pass judgement it's time to listen. 'Will used to get very uptight,' says Richards, who was not always his captain's biggest fan. 'Now he is much more relaxed. He has a word for everyone. He is much better for that.'

Deano has a bigger say in what goes on this season. So too have the other senior players. Now, when England tried this sort of approach before, albeit in an unplanned and unstructured way, they came completely off the rails. Remember Murrayfield 1990? A Grand Slam for the taking? One of the abiding images of that match is of England wracked by indecision. At one point Carling called up Simon Hodgkinson for a kick at goal. Too late. Brian Moore had already grabbed the ball and set the forwards rumbling towards the Scottish goal line. They never got there.

Was there not a danger of a similar thing happening here? Was there not a risk of the captain's authority being undermined? 'That's old hat,' says Rowell. 'The captain shouldn't have to go and pick up the ball every time there's a penalty kick. He needs sub-managers. In rugby there arc a lot of moving parts, so the players must be physically, mentally and technically fit enough to take their own decisions in split seconds.'

It's a sign of Carling's own refound self-confidence that he did not feel at all threatened by the dispersal of influence. 'You can only go so far with a team by telling them,' he says. 'To win the World Cup we shall need leaders throughout the side. That's not captaincy by committee but co-ordination.'

And it works. As England have sought to evolve a more complex game plan, appropriate to whatever situation might confront them, be it the dervish Irish or the imaginative instincts of the French, so they needed a more sophisticated, yet clearly delineated chain of command. 'It's imperative that the forwards play well, so there's got to be a leader,' says Brian Moore. 'Dean is a voice of wisdom. He cuts through the verbiage. Mine's a primary view as hooker. Will's is the overview. But both of us rely on 8, 9 and 10 for the practicalities. They have to adapt and not attempt things that are not on.'

For the first time ever coaches have been allowed on to the field of play at half-time this year with a view to amending the team tactics for the second half. Not everyone in the game approved of the move, fearing that it would lead to even more robotic rugby, the movements of players dictated not by inclination and reactive insight, but by the play book in the coach's back pocket. At half-time in England's opening championship match at Lansdowne Road, Jack Rowell wandered on to the pitch towards the huddle of players. Big, strong words from the big man? No, he cocked an ear, listened and wandered back off again. 'I was happy with what was happening,' said Rowell later. 'I want the mood where there can be no backsliding, where they know they are responsible, self-reliant. I'm leading from the back. I want the captain leading at the front.'

And so he has done, right through to that quickly-aborted lap of honour at Twickenham. He has relished the trust placed in him by Jack Rowell and found a new appetite for the rigours of rugby once again. Although perhaps a touch overstated, there was perhaps some truth in Stuart Barnes's comments. Carling did not perform for Quins in those early days of the season with anything like the majesty, pomp or even energy which has characterised his play for England. But Will Carling is no Brian Moore, a man who makes every training session a competitive battle.

In a position which demands a certain sharpness and keen edge, it would be impossible to expect a player such as Carling to maintain peak form throughout the year. We perhaps also expect too much of a man who has the demands and profile of England captain to contend with

That new Carling magic: Carling shows that the old snap and hunger have returned as he takes on the Welsh defence in Cardiff.

The best of rivals: There was talk of animosity dating back to the Lions tour of 1993, which both players denied, but there's no doubt-ing the bruising intent of Gavin Hastings as he closes in on his old adversary.

as well, albeit that profile has been sharpened by himself and to his own advantage. One man who might have been expected to have little time for any prima donna behaviour from Carling was former England coach Dick Best, now Director of Coaching at Harlequins. Best had yet to take over the reins at the Stoop when the Barnes arti-cle appeared, but he maintained close contact with the club during his three years in the England post.

He had known Carling since he first came to London as a student back in 1988 and was his club coach in those formative years. Best might rightly have felt a certain bitterness at being dumped by England. If he did, he certainly didn't take it out on Carling. Best has a reputa-tion for a sharp tongue, particularly for those players he feels are not pulling their weight. Significantly, given all those possible premises for resentment, he has not a bad word to say about Will Carling.

'He had mere boys around him at Harlequins in the first part of the season,' says Best. 'And it showed. Will sets himself very high standards and he perhaps found it difficult to come to terms with it when those around were not coming up to scratch. Remember too that a lot of his old muckers – Halliday, Ackford,

was hemmed in a corner and people were jabbing fingers in his chest telling him where England were going wrong. Will is actually a relatively shy bloke and hates all this sort of fuss. What people respond too though is the myth of Will Carling: they relate to his position as England captain, not to the bloke himself.'

Carling is much more at home taking solitary walks on the moors and dabbling in a spot of oil painting than he is showboating around the West End. He still has a fondness too for aspects of his former military life. He has, on occasions, taken a few of the England squad along with him to SAS headquarters in Hereford. Carling is much more at ease with his background now. And he is much more at one with himself on the field, per-haps because he's been reacquainted with his old partner Jeremy Guscott, restored after a year's lay-off with injury. The impression of the season has been of Guscott not quite hitting that beauti-fully wafting pose which sees him floating past defenders. Whatever the reality may be about Guscott's abilities, it is no coincidence that Carling has enjoyed such a good run at the pre-cise moment that the Bath centre is back along-side him.

'We've got a great attacking full-back now and Jerry's back,' is how Carling weighs up the

What people respond too though is the myth of Will Carling: they relate to his position as England captain, not to the bloke himself.

threat from England's three-quarters this season. 'That means the opposition now have to look at a number of options that England can throw at them. Jerry makes space for all sorts of people around him. He's a genuine threat – a world-class per-former. People are far more worried about him than they are about me. In turn that gives me more room.'

Carling the man is con-tent, so too is Carling the

Winterbottom and Skinner – had all retired.

'I've certainly never had any doubts about Will's commitment to the club. I don't think many people actually understand just what sort of pressure he comes under. I was in a pub with him in Richmond, which is a rare occurrence for Will, about 18 months ago. All of a sudden he

player and Carling the captain. 'Now I don't have to spend time thinking about every aspect of play, which is a big help to my own game,' he says. 'I can go out and play.'

And so he did. He was not alone in finding new directions and fresh stimulus during England's record breaking season.

the Old guard

Rob Andrew is the world's most capped fly-half. He can also lay claim to another record – the world's most rubbished fly-half. For what seemed like years he was criticised for being dull, negative, cautious, inhibited, lacking in sparkle and imagination. Apart from that he wasn't a bad player.

Fortunately Rob Andrew is also one of the world's most equitable blokes. Not a soft touch (he was born in Yorkshire, after all), rather one who is remarkably even tempered and even handed, one with deep reserves of self-belief. And he can fight. He is never daunted by the odds and he will do everything in his power to get the edge on an opponent. Have you ever seen him shirk a challenge, duck a tackle, buckle in the face of pressure? No, and this is why Rob Andrew has probably had his most successful twelve months since he first laced up a pair of rugby boots.

It's ironic that his purple patch has come at a time when he might perhaps have breathed a sigh of relief, turned down the competitive fires and coasted for a few months. Just under a year ago, aged 31, he was approaching 60 caps for his country and had finally shaken off Barnes who had dogged his footsteps for the best part of a decade, who, by being the point of contrast, had prompted much of the criticism levelled at Andrew. Barnes was everything that Andrew was not. Maverick, socialist, loud, opinionated, bohemian and, in life as well as on a rugby pitch, a free spirit. The terms of the debate had long been drawn up, the followers long taken to their different camps. Barnes ran with the ball, Andrew did not. Barnes played off the top of his head, Andrew played by numbers. When Andrew was dropped two years ago to make way for Barnes to play against Scotland, it seemed as if those in the red corner had been vindicated. England, with Barnes calling the shots, ran free at Twickenham, Guscott and the Underwoods had a field day, and the crowd rose to acclaim a new dawn for England.

What had happened a few months later? Andrew was back in harness for the British Lions, orchestrating that historic victory over the All Blacks in the second Test. Great fighters are the ones who get back up from the canvas. Great men are not those who have never known adver-

54

sity, but those who know what to do when it hits them.

At the end of the South African tour, Barnes was history and the rivalry was dead. Barnes's retirement meant that Rob Andrew was now unchallenged for his position in the England no. 10 shirt, so far ahead of any other contenders that he could put his feet up and relax. Of course he never saw it like that, immediately nodding in agreement with those on the touchline eager for a new angle on an old story who began to talk up the prospects of Mike Catt. 'Great player,' they said. 'Full of talent and potential, can read a game, is brash, tough, able to spot a gap, runs like a stag, floats like a butterfly, has a great

party trick when he turns invisible at the first sight of an openside flanker, has four legs, three hands, can kick 100 metres with his little toe . . .'

Catt had the lot and was sure to put Andrew in his place within a few months. All nonsense of course, but we all said it and Rob Andrew agreed. (Catt is a fine player as his form at the back for England has shown but he had proved nothing up to that point at stand-off.)

Andrew though saw the challenge and set out to meet it. He has trained harder than ever. As with the others of his generation – Moore, Richards and Rory Underwood – Rob realised the truth of that adage which has accompanied all those great sportsmen and women who have

Swing high, sweet boot: Rob Andrew follows through as yet another successful penalty attempt flies between the posts against Romania.

defied the calender. 'You know you can do it,' runs the saying, 'but can you do it again?'

Motivation is the key to longevity. The arrival of Jack Rowell came at the perfect time for Rob Andrew (and, as we have seen, for Will Carling as well). Jack, by his very presence, never mind his manner, represented a new challenge. Rowell also brought with him fresh ways of thinking and a different outlook on how to play the game. Rob took it all in his stride. And he began to play like . . . er, Stuart Barnes?

A more spiteful man would cut off your nose for suggesting such a comparison. But Rob Andrew is not like that. He would merely smile at the notion that his style of play these last nine months bears something of a resemblance to his old adversary and simply lay before you a few of his own observations on the subject. 'I've always been like this,' he says. 'Remember Cambridge?'

Well, that was over ten years ago. What happened in between? Rob will accept in part that opening the game up has not always been his priority not, as he sees it, because he lacked the ability to do so, but because it did not suit England's strengths to do that.' We had a great set piece side for several seasons and so it would have been madness not to play to them,' says

Andrew. 'They have gone now, the laws have changed, so there is a need for a different approach.'

Andrew though also confided one very telling thing to me on his return from playing club rugby in Toulouse three years ago. There, he had played some wonderfully carefree rugby, full of dash and verve, often triggering attacks from well inside his own half. Why? 'I have a natural tendency to fit in with those around me,' he said. 'An inclination to suppress my own desires in the better interest of others. What's best for the group is best for me. At Toulouse I was happy to go with their way of doing things. With England, the ways were just different.'

This season Andrew has moved towards the ways of Rowell and Cusworth, a shift in keeping with his own assessment of what will be needed to win the the World Cup 'The side who wins will be the one with the best all-round game,' he says. 'Ground conditions are so good that you're not going to be able to slog it out up front. That's the big lesson we learnt from our summer tour of South Africa. Our asscts also have changed, from the solid strength of Teague, Dooley and Skinner to the dynamic, ball handling attributes of Clarke, Rodber and Ubogu. It makes sense to involve them more.'

Les Cusworth has encouraged Andrew to get his back line standing flatter, to play 'up in their face' as Cusworth puts it. England's opening try of the championship against Ireland would never have happened under the old regime. A quick ball from the line-out, Andrew stands flat and hits Carling with a deft short pass on the gain line. Through the England captain goes and England have laid down their marker for the season. 'If you watched the games in South Africa we actually began to develop the style then,' says Andrew. 'We get the backs across the gain line and get the forwards back into the game more rapidly. The game worldwide has moved on. The southern hemisphere sides have taken it on again significantly. You only have to see last year's Bledisloe Cup to recognise that and if we don't compete with that we will be blown away. It is much more physical and far more skilful. There is more action, more movement. It is, in truth, far more enjoyable.'

Enjoyable even though Rob Andrew invariably begins his work day as a chartered surveyor and associate director of DTZ Debenham Thorpe at 7:30 a.m. so that he can fit in all his commitments, escaping to the gym if necessary in his lunch hour, or to the athletics track or training at Wasps in good time in the evening. Five days a week, there is no escape. On the sixth day he played rugby and on the seventh he . . . probably had to pitch up to an England training session. Then there's home in north London and a young family to cope with. How does he keep all the

The man they love to hate: Brian Moore strikes the pose, here to salute victory over Wales, which has infuriated so many opponents.

balls in the air? 'When I leave the office and I'm on the pitch I really have to leave it all behind and put everything into the game. I try to work hard and play hard. After a weekend of rugby I'm rather glad to be getting on the Tube again to go into the office.'

Oh, by the way – Andrew also kicks goals. In all the focus on England's evolution towards a more rounded game, and Andrew's central role in that, the fact that he's been banging over goals at will can sometimes be taken as read. Behind every ball soaring towards the posts however lies a bucket of sweat, hours and hours on the practice ground and a man called Dave Alred.

Andrew was handed the position of principal goalkicker for England just over a year ago. He'd always had a boot on him and had often performed well for Wasps as well as for England.

But now the job was all his. How did he respond? You've got it – out there late at night, long after everyone else has headed for the comforting warmth of the shower and bar, there was Rob Andrew teeing another one up. In exactly the same way as Nick Faldo strove for perfection by dismantling his more than adequate golf swing and remodelling it under the tutelage of David Leadbetter, so Andrew stripped his action down to its basics and started again with help from the only specialist kicking coach in the world, Dave Alred. The result? Take your pick

The pain and the strain: Rob Andrew and Brian Moore get to grips with each other as the preparation for yet another arduous season gets under way.

from: a record 27 points in that historic victory in the first test over South Africa, 10 out of 11 successes against Romania, the full house against Canada to equal Didier Camberabero's world record of 30 points, a hatful more against Scotland to win the Grand Slam to take Andrew past Jon Webb's record aggregate of points for England.

To the naive eye, Andrew's style looks much like anyone else's and not very different from before. But it is different. There has been a radical overhaul. 'All we've done is to make the kick more technically efficient,' explains Andrew. 'Round-the-corner kickers tend to sweep into the ball and therefore run the danger of hooking. What Dave has tried to do with me is to make me follow through straight once I have hit the ball. It's basically like a golf swing. The key to good goal-kicking is that it should not matter which side of the field you kick from because the line of the ball is dead straight.'

And so on many a dreary Sunday morning in winter, when his body cried out for rest, Rob Andrew would pack himself off down the M4 to Bristol for a couple of hours tutorial with Alred. On the back of such dedication are Grand Slams won.

Andrew is not alone, of course, in putting in all the hours in search of success. It's easy to appreciate just how fulfilling it might be when Grand Slams are acclaimed, but when the reality of all the hours pledged is confronted it's unlikely that many people would have the inclination to go through with it all, no matter what their potential might be. Yet the older some of the guys get, the more of it they seem to want. Carling has rebutted suggestions that he might retire after the World Cup, Andrew says that he is enjoying it so much that 'to give up after the World Cup would be a very difficult thing to do,' Underwood has come out of retirement, Richards would play every day of the week if it meant that he did not have have to train, while Moore has eyes on the Lions tour of 1997.

only as long as there are enough victories to sustain you. If I'd lived through England's unproductive era of the Seventies and Eighties, I'd have gone long ago.'

In fact Moore is perceptive enough to see that he will not really know how long he will actually carry on because he has no idea how the events of the next couple of months will affect him. 'I rely on feeling more than thought when assessing my motivation,' he said over a pint in the Harlequins clubhouse a week after the Grand Slam had been won. 'You don't really know how you're going to feel so there's no point making too many firm statements.'

Brian Moore is such an honest character (which is why he said what he did after the Scotland match, much to the overblown annoyance of those who would rather sportsmen behaved like politicians when it came to calling a situation as it really is) that he would never dream of playing on if he weren't fully committed to the cause. But Moore's importance to England goes beyond the rage with which he fills a white shirt, a rage which has enabled him to compete on level terms with the world's leading hookers who are all three stones heavier than him.

Moore's brain is every bit as sharp as his tongue. There are many players who can headbang their way through a game. Moore is not like that. He may play with passion but he plays with poise and subtlety as well. If the forward game needs tilting a degree or two one way in the course of a match Moore has the vision as well as the calmness of mind to recognise it and bring it about. He has marshalled the England pack superbly for the past five years. Without him to direct operations England would have fallen apart far more often than they have done in recent times.

Even though he has pledged his desire to make one more Lions tour, to South Africa in 1997, his third in all, Moore does wonder whether the fires within him will still be burning by then, particularly if England were to win the World Cup. 'I think I'll still want a piece of the action,' he said, 'but I don't know that I will. You've got to have goals and if we were to win, then how would I feel? I'll have done it all, or will I? I don't really, really know. I feel as good

At arm's length: Dean Richards seen in a classic scene, holding off the French intruder, Olivier Roumat, with one arm while presenting the perfect ball to Ben Clarke with the other.

Moore has epitomised the hard edge which has framed English rugby in the nineties. There's far more to this than the snarling pitbull expression, taped forehead and clenched fists of caricature (one which, admittedly, Brian is happy to cultivate). What you see is but a small part of the whole. The hard men are those who can cope inside with what is going on around them, not those who raise their fists occasionally. In this Brain Moore is almost without equal in the English if not the world game. He is a man with a desperate need to win, quite befitting the character once described by Dick Best as: 'the sort who would turn a game of snap into a contact sport.'

Moore, it should be said, is also a bit of a softie, regularly doing unpublicised work for charity, to whom he donated the monies won in a libel case against Stuart Barnes last year. But enough of dismantling the image: let's hear what makes the pitbull take to the rugby field. 'There are few opportunities in life to match yourself in direct physical battle against someone else,' says Moore. 'Opportunities which are socially acceptable that is. A lot of people don't need that release. I do. But the winning is vital. Taking part in itself is not enough. Each 80 minutes is unique. That's why you come back for more. But

as I've ever felt that's for sure but, I must admit, it is increasingly difficult to keep it all going. I seriously wonder whether an international rugby player will be able to hold down a high intensity job in five years time.'

Moore, a commercial litigation partner with a firm of London solicitors, Edward Lewis & Co, manages it all now through good time-management. If the game were to go professional, which Moore believes it will and should, it would make no difference to him at all. 'Contrary to what many people may believe about me,' says Moore, 'I couldn't give a toss about money. I've got a good job. It's the principle of the thing which is important. There's money in the game, lots of it, and the players have a right to a share of it.'

Moore has never taken a step back, on or off the field. He does concede, however, that his timing may have been at fault when speaking out after the Scotland match only because the furore took some of the sheen off the Grand Slam achievement although, in the same breath, he holds to the truth of every word he says: 'Funny to think that I might have brought devolution a step nearer.'

If Moore is defined by his loud presence then you only have to move a couple of rows back in the scrum to find his exact counterpoint. Dean Richards is a great, intimidating slab of silence; a man of few words and huge actions. In many quarters Richards is the most popular man in the modern game, adored for the contradiction that he is. One whose shambling, socks-down, Just William appearance is at odds with the fact that he is never caught out by being in the wrong place at the wrong time. A man who hates training yet would willingly play six days a week. He is respected throughout the land for his uncomplaining nature which sees him absorb eye-watering punishment on the field and then often dash from the shower so as to be in time for night duty at Hinckley police station where he works in the motorway response unit. Richards is happiest far

Still together after all these years: Rory Underwood joins his younger brother, Tony, for an early morning jog at England's New Year training camp in Lanzarote.

away from the television lights and notebooks of the media with his young family, or clay-pigeon shooting or with a couple of mates in a local pub downing a few pints of Theakston's Old Peculiar. Far from his public image, he is a man of great wit, charm and warmth. He is also regarded as one of the most indispensable men in the England pack.

Not that they haven't tried to dispense with him. They have, most woundingly in the World Cup of 1991 when he made way in the quarter-final for Mickey Skinner. Again this season Jack Rowell dabbled with the notion of leaving him on the sidelines, omitting him for the Romania match. Psychology on the part of Rowell? Who knows? Several of the side actually apologised to Deano in private, a remarkable state of affairs. He is a special man though. 'When the rough stuff starts you want to look round and see Deano there,' says Brian Moore. 'He is utterly dependable, trustworthy. What he does is very hard, usually unseen and invariably unappreciated. Running with the ball is visible; getting it is not.'

Richards himself is uncomfortable with the demands on the modern player. There is more to the game for him than the mere 80 minutes on the pitch. But the modern game cannot do without him. Even though many wrote him off as being too lumpy, too set in his ways for the dynamic rhythms in fashion today, he has proved conclusively that England do not perform anything like as effectively without him. Having Richards at the core allows Ben Clarke and Tim Rodber to set off on those damaging runs.

Geoff Cooke called him 'a colossus'; Jack Rowell describes him as 'immense'; his teammates call him 'awesome'. Does anybody out there object? Silence . . .

Glad that he's back: Rory Underwood races clear of the Romanian defence to show just why the England management were so delighted when he reversed his decision to retire.

the modern *player*

I t's not the sort of thing you would want to pin to your bedroom wall for fear of waking and realising with a cold sweat that it wasn't all a nightmare. The fitness chart, as the players know only too well, is for real. Every day is marked out: train, rest or play. The rhythm is simple, the routine set. There is no escape. If you want to make the World Cup, then the line has to be toed.

There was a time in the not too distant past, maybe even as late as the last World Cup, when corners could be cut and a full-blown commitment to fitness training avoided. Now there is nowhere to hide. You only had to see how poorly the French performed in this year's Five Nations to appreciate how fine the line is between achievement and failure. The French are still nothing like as structured and systematic in their approach to physical conditioning, relying on native wit and the rigours of their domestic club championship to get themselves in shape. On tour, as they showed in New Zealand last summer, they have the time and opportunity – and in Pierre Berbizier, the perfect taskmaster –

to put things right. But this year the much trumpeted backrow of Cabannes, Benetton and Benazzi were yards off their expected pace. Cabannes, the outstanding openside of recent years, was dropped for the Irish match.

The English, as befits the national character, are more thorough and disciplined. It was Geoff Cooke who put the house in order. Rugby players always took a self-deluding pride in their macho ability to tough it out, to believe somehow that drinking a few pints every night didn't matter, that an English fry-up on the morning of the game was necessary ballast for the battles ahead, that being physically hard and intimidating during the 80 minutes could more than compensate for a few training sessions missed during the week. Cooke changed that mentality. In fact he ridiculed those who thought the demands impossible by pointing to other amateur sports such as rowing and swimming where ordinary club standard athletes put in two or three times the amount of training as a matter of course, often at horribly anti-social hours.

Rugby was forced to sit up and take notice.

Hence the birth of the dreaded wall chart, detailing times to focus on speed, or stamina, or strength. Diet sheets, ergometers, plyometrics – never mind the routine of a rugby player changing, the whole language changed. The system has been in place for a few years now and is an accepted part of an international player's life, if not always loved. Jeff Probyn, the Wasps prop, used to hang his clothes on his ergometer, reckoning that to be the only fit and proper use for a rowing machine. Dean Richards has never made any secret of his dislike of the relentless monotony of training, not to mention the inroads it makes on one's time. 'The level of commitment is pushing things to the limit,' says Richards. 'If, when I first started playing for England in 1986, I had to do the things I do now, I could not have carried on my career as a policeman. When you

look at the weekends away, the training nights and the phone calls, the demands are horrendous.'

Tom McNab, who once coached Daley Thompson, was appointed fitness advisor by Cooke. He taught the England players about stride patterns, soft jaws, high knee lifts and, that technological invention, running spikes. Few, if any, rugby players had ever ventured near an athletics track for training. Now most of them do at some time or another. White meat was in, red meat was out; strange things began to be seen in the hands of players after matches – jugs of orange juice rather than ten pints of foaming best bitter, the normal prelude to another fading ritual of a Saturday night, a vindaloo curry. All gone. Well, not quite. The boys do sneak away for the odd session now and again, but there's no doubt

A break in the routine: England escaped to the sun of Lanzarote at New Year to put the finishing touches to their Five Nations preparation.

When you look at the weekends away, the training nights and the phone calls, the demands are horrendous.

for the players to fit in with their specific needs and situations. The first thing Leicester flanker Neil Back did on hearing of his selection for the World Cup squad was not to go out and crack open the champagne with his mates but to ring Rex and get a new fitness programme.

that the social habits of the players have changed enormously.

Nowadays it is Rex Hazeldine at Loughborough University who sets the tempo. He designs both long and short term schedules

How do they fit it all in? With great difficulty in some cases. Tim Rodber has stepped back from active duties with his battalion, the Green Howards, so as to concentrate on a big twelve month push on rugby. Dewi Morris gave up his job as a sales executive while Jason Leonard was happy to swap the sapping labours of the building site where he was a carpenter for

a job in a suit. As Brian Moore was saying, it's unlikely that someone such as surgeon Jon Webb would ever be able, even now, to combine two demanding sporting and professional careers.

Several players – Ben Clarke, Jeremy Guscott and Mike Catt for example – have managed to negotiate positions which have flexible time built in to their contracts so as to enable them to meet all training requirements, be it with England or the club. Clarke, who works in public relations and education for National Power, is often to be seen at the crack of dawn heading up the hill towards Bath University. There he joins in with several other Bath colleagues for a gruelling 90 minute session alongside top athletes from other sports under the guidance of the university's head of sport, Ged Roddy. 'If players turn up at 6:30 a.m. before their day's work, and find that it's sheer drudgery, then they won't come again,' says Roddy. 'We have to keep variety in the ses-

sions to maintain their interest. The trick is to let them have rests. We do a maximum of 20 minutes at a time in which we might work, for example, on developing power over four or five metres. Obviously the forwards and backs do slightly different things.'

Leaping over hurdles, hitting punch bags, bounding, sidestepping through cones, and all before the milk has been delivered. It's a far cry from the days when the likes of those legendary Irishmen Moss Keane and Willie Duggan used to warm up for internationals with fifteen pints of Guinness the night before and a fag before running out on to the pitch.

Variety is the key if players are not to be completely flattened by the sheer repetitiveness of it all – play, get bruised, recover, train, get wet, find some dry kit, make it to the gym in lunch hour – particularly here in the northern hemisphere where the season is much longer than in Australia, New Zealand or South Africa. And, for the most parts, the winters are harsher.

England though, in this the longest of all seasons, stretching through (or so England hope) to the World Cup final on 24 June, have decided to add to their considerable work load. In autumn the players themselves decided to meet every fortnight at Marlow, Bucks, a convenient mid-point between Bath, London and Leicester, for training sessions. The thinking was that in 1991 the nucleus of the side had been together for a few years and, as a result, knew each other's strengths and weaknesses well and had nurtured that elusive, intangible but so important quality, team spirit.

In the preceding twelve to eighteen months, several new faces had popped up in the England squad. The twice-monthly meets were a means to bring everyone together, on and off the field. The confident, co-ordinated manner of England's opening fifteen minutes against Ireland left no one in any doubt as to the benefits of it all. However, the line is very fine between asking just enough of players and demanding too much.

Just ten days after England won the Grand Slam they were back in those same Marlow fields, training and plotting. And then again a fortnight later, and again and . . . Throw in a couple of weekend gatherings before the squad were to depart for South Africa in mid-May and the

players will have seen more of other than their wives or girlfriends. There comes a point when the whole operation, designed to foster unity and understanding, threatens to become counter-productive. 'To be honest, I get a bit bored with so much talk,' said Brian Moore.

Rowell, sharp operator that he is, will no doubt have something up his sleeve to keep old sweats such as Moore and Richards fresh and eager. He knows full well that it would be madness to treat the pair in the same way as new-comers such as Kyran Bracken or Mike Catt.

For them every sighting of a rugby ball at an England training session must still be a thing of wonder: wonder that everything is going so swimmingly well and that they are both very much at the sharp end of the whole marvellous show. Of course neither of them would doubt

their own abilities for a minute – and nor should they have any reason to – but even so making the position your own is a very different thing from wanting and hoping to do so. This season both Bracken and Catt have made definite, long-term claims on the no. 9 and no. 15 shirts respectively.

Last summer Bracken was just another brow-beaten student, sweating and fretting over his law exams. He took the risk of opting out of England's tour to South Africa in order to sit his finals. The gamble paid off. He is now a trainee solicitor with Alsters in Bristol and is firmly established ahead of Dewi Morris as England's scrum-half. He was left out against Romania but, much to his surprise, was called to the colours for the Canadian game. He took the opportunity with both hands, scoring his maiden

international try. 'For Jack to make changes after Romania was a bit of a shock,' says Bracken. 'I'd had an operation on my knee and then I didn't go to South Africa. It turned out to be my sort of game though against Canada with a lot of expansive rugby.'

Bracken – young, articulate, good looking – is a prototype of the modern international. He has come up through the system so that, to him, regular fitness tests against a battery of electronic gadgetry, is normal. He expects to have to shape his time carefully to fit in his dual commit-

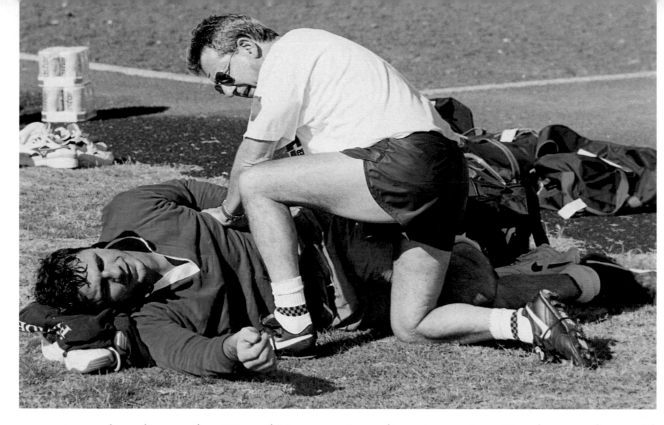

ments to work and to rugby. His ambition to reach the very top is shown by his attention to detail. Once at the summit, Bracken set about improving himself still further. Last autumn the RFU brought in former Bath and England scrum-half Richard Hill to sharpen Bracken's pass. The result was not a bit of spit and polish but a complete overhaul. Bracken dismantled his old action, attempting now to flick rather than swing the ball away. 'It's a push away with the wrists, rather than bringing the whole body into it,' he explains. 'It will take a long time for me to adopt it properly, probably two or three seasons.'

And so indeed it seemed from some of his hesitant, somewhat uneven performances at the base of the scrum this season. His old pass was a thing of some fluency. Yet in order to make himself better still he gambled. Such is the attitude of the young generation.

Mike Catt is of the same generation but different roots to Bracken. Catt was born in Port Elizabeth, South Africa, of an English mother. In a few years he has come from nowhere (with all due respect to Port Elizabeth) to stand on the threshold of perhaps becoming one of the outstanding players of the 1995 World Cup. He is that good, full of talent and presence.

When he first pitched up at Bath – he was on holiday at his uncle's and tried Gloucester first but no one answered the phone – he made an immediate impression. Not because he could run, pass, kick and all that sort of stuff. Dozens of youngsters turn up at the Recreation Ground who can do all that. No, Catt made his mark because he had the right attitude: mentally tough, resilient with a touch of cockiness. 'He got stuck in and got his hands dirty, which always goes down well here,' says Bath coach Brian Ashton.

Catt's innate confidence and sense of himself was shown in the remarkable ease with which he slotted into the full-back position. He had played little senior rugby of note as a full-back when he was called on as a replacement against Canada for the unfortunate Paul Hull. Hull must have been in more pain from watching Catt score two tries that afternoon than he was from his own injury. Catt has been there ever since in wonderful form, so much so that, despite being the outstanding player on England's tour last summer, Hull has been left out of the World Cup party. 'Mike Catt has given one of the best all-round displays of football I've ever seen,' said Jack Rowell when the 26 man World Cup squad was announced. 'It's very, very bad luck on Paul Hull who did so well for us last year.'

Catt too is a new-age player. Rugby has found him an occupation as marketing executive with Johnson's News Group in Bath, the company which employs several other players from the club. Of course there is still work to be done. 'If

I can't do my job,' says Catt, 'then the company will soon find someone else who can.'

Nonetheless the job does offer scope to combine work and what used to be called play, now called modern rugby. There are commercial opportunities also for these players to compensate them for the time they have to take off from their jobs.

The England squad formed their own company to look after their commercial activities at the time of the last World Cup. It was all a bit of a shambles and the players were lucky if they cleared £1,000 each. Now the whole operation is much smoother. A representative of Parallel Media, the company which now acts for them, travelled round South Africa with them last summer with a view to negotiating deals for the World Cup there this summer. Last season the players took home, after tax and deductions, about £6,000 a man. Several of them though

also have other personal deals, for advertising, after-dinner speaking and newspaper columns (nine of them are signed up with different papers) which might earn them several thousand pounds more. This year all the players should take a minimum of £8-10,000. This may well sound a decent return from an amateur sport but in fact is still behind the monies on offer down in the southern hemisphere where the Wallaby World Cup squad have signed a contract which guarantees them £35,000.

Despite what many diehard amateurs on club committees throughout the land might think, money is the last thing on the minds of the players at the moment. For them this year has not been about bank accounts but about tackle bags, scrum machines and multi-gyms. The thought in all their minds was simple: to win the Five Nations and go off to the World Cup in the best possible order. And that is exactly what they did.

the Coming together

I t sounded very grand indeed. Lots of running, loads of passes, integrate here, pressurise there: a nice, neat, sophisticated game plan. So much for the theory. Would it work?

It's all very well to look back now in admiration at how smoothly it's all gone and forget about all the possible pitfalls along the way. How would the squad react to Jack Rowell, for starters? Big men with big ideas don't always hit it off with big men with proven reputations.

Will Carling was under threat for his place, Jerry Guscott was still a doubtful starter after twelve months sidelined with a troublesome pelvic injury. Even if he were to return would it necessarily be at the expense of Phil de Glanville? Carling was not playing that well at Harlequins, de Glanville was a Bath man, so too was Rowell. Plenty to ponder there.

And then there was this game plan. What if it didn't come off? What if the winds blew, the rain catted and dogged, the pitch squelched, the opposition scored first – then what? Revert to type, hoof the leather of it and hope that Rob

Andrew kicked some goals?

Yes, there were plenty of imponderables. To England's great, great credit, they came through all of them unscathed. Whatever they may have said at the time, it was vitally important that they came through as Grand Slam champions. They might possibly have been able to rationalise a brilliant French victory at Twickenham along the lines that the gods for once blessed *les tricolores* and let them run riot with their flowing rugby. Even so, a home defeat would have jolted the confidence and, as they were all aware, self-belief is the essential prerequisite to success. You need to be more than merely lucky to win a World Cup tournament; you need to do more than just hope you're going to win it. You have to know you're going to win it.

But win the Five Nations they did. 'It was important to go off to South Africa unbeaten,' said Rob Andrew. 'We played down the significance of it during the championship itself, but it was important. Now we're in the right frame of mind knowing there's work to be done

76

but confident we can do it.'

There used to be a time when a November international fixture was an exception, played only when there was a touring party in the Isles. Now it is the norm, as a warm-up to the Five Nations championship. This year there was to be a warm-up to the warm-up.

For Rowell, the Romania match was the perfect opportunity to test his new charges. He had been none too impressed at times when watching from his distanced position in South Africa. If these men meant business, now was their chance to show it.

Romania had given Wales a tough time in Bucharest in their World Cup qualifying match in September. But since then much had changed. (Since then we've found out a thing or two about Wales as well.) Romania, once a substantial force in the understrata of European rugby, have had since the Revolution an alarming tendency to behave and perform like complete novices. Too much of a heady dose of freedom gone to their heads? God forbid, for if ever a country deserved to be liberated from a madman, Romania did. No, the malaise was simply a

classic case of selectorial incompetence.

The Romanian federation sent over a bunch of raw youngsters to tackle the might of England with a view to preparing for the future. Jack Rowell knows that the future always begins right here and now and sent out his strongest possible team. The only surprise was the omission of Richards, which may or may not have just been a bit of psychological kidology on the part of Rowell. You never quite know with big Jack, which is just the way he likes it.

Even back in November the England manager was well aware of the World Cup clock already ticking down. He wanted every last second of real practice time. And so Jeremy Guscott was thrown into the deep end and told to swim. He swam.

Guscott is one of the great talents in any sport. Like Muhammad Ali or George Best, he has a touch and timing which are way beyond the reach of mere mortals. As his Bath and England team-mate Simon Halliday once said of Guscott's powers of acceleration: 'It's nothing as crude as a change of pace. He just seems to float away.'

Sadly the butterfly had been winged, and

grievously. At the start of the previous season Guscott was continually hampered by a groin problem. Rest would cure it, they said. And then more rest. And yet more. It never did heal throughout that arid season when Guscott's uplifting play was sorely missed. A place was kept open for him for the South African tour. The plane took off without him. Would he ever play again? 'It will happen,' he said in that languid way of his. 'It might be in two months' time or two years' time, but it will happen.'And so it did. The rest, along with an operation, intensive physiotherapy and many consultations, eventually worked. Guscott could play again. Or could he?

Just because he had finally scrambled clear of the treatment table and out into the training pitch, taking knocks, trading passes and selling dummies, did not mean that he could still actually do it out where and when it really counted. A whole posse of media decamped to the northern outpost of West Hartlepool to witness the second coming. It took fifteen minutes for the great man to touch the ball. Long before the end he was blowing, as were Bath for that matter committing an act of grand larceny in escaping with a 20-18 victory.

It was enough for Rowell anyway, who pitched him straight into the international arena.

Rough n' tumble: Jerry Guscott shirked nothing on his comeback from injury, here tangling with Ireland's Niall Hogan and Niall Woods.

sons. But were we really seeing the same Guscott, the arch tormentor and teaser of defences, the guy who made it all look so easy?

There was nothing wrong with his defence (and never has been, just to emphasise the point for those dullards who, perhaps through some sort of closet racism, have snidely whispered from time to time that the glamour boy might lack bottle in the tackle). But the nagging feeling persisted at the end of the Five Nations that the full ease of movement, the full burn of acceleration, was not quite there. Or, perhaps it was and is, but only against the stopwatch. Guscott may well be as fast as he ever was, but speed is of the mind as well as the body.

At the highest level it is the split second not the second which differentiates the good from

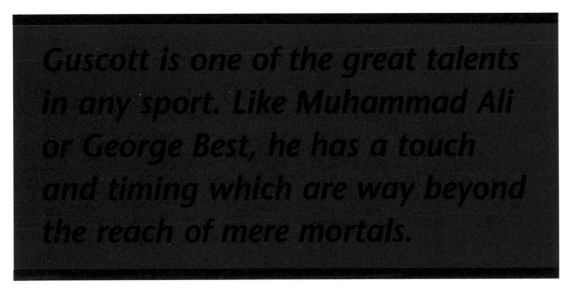

Guscott is one of the great talents in any sport. Like Muhammad Ali or George Best, he has a touch and timing which are way beyond the reach of mere mortals.

Guscott saw the season through, unhampered it seemed by his injury. He played in every match and missed none of Bath's games for medical rea-

A new strike force: Unfortunate as it was for Paul Hull, injured against Canada, Mike Catt's arrival into the full-back slot brought an extra dimension to England's back play.

the very good. And then there is the need for the athlete to believe, very deeply indeed, way beyond even what the medics and the clipboards tell you, that the abilities are unimpaired. There were occasions this season, particularly against Scotland, when Guscott made a break but did not finish it off in that wonderfully casual way of his. It was not that his legs seemed to have gone; it was worse than that. His arrogance seemed to have gone.

Bath boy, which is the essential reason why he has never taken the rugby league bait, all the hundreds of thousands of pounds of it, to head north. 'What they offered me, did not turn me on,' says Guscott.

Ever since he was a young mini rugby player at the club, Guscott had always played Jack the Lad about his talents, mickey-taking on the field and in the dressing-room. He says he's happy with his comeback, and we must leave it at that.

Guscott has never had any doubt about his own abilities. He has been known to tell a few people about them from time to time. However, no matter what the fashion catwalk, on which he occasionally appears, may suggest, he is no prima donna. There may be an aloof air about him, there may even be times when he cuts you dead with a look, but he is essentially one of the boys. He spends time at the bar with the forwards, not the backs 'He likes the Sumo mentality, although he isn't one,' says John Hall, captain and veteran of Bath.

Guscott, a former bricklayer, now pursuing a serious career with British Gas, albeit one structured to allow him time off, is a home-loving

The criticism of his play is of the finest degree. He has been class this season, but not world-class. Of course it's no mere coincidence that the man alongside him, Will Carling, has hit those heights, proving perhaps that as long as the partnership is working, as long as one is creating for the other, then it does not matter who gets the plaudits. The prospect of Guscott back to his disdainful best in the World Cup is one of the great mouth-watering attractions of the tournament.

Rowell must have been delighted that Guscott came through that first game against Romania unscathed. He was less happy, even though England ran out victors by 54-3, at the number of chances which went begging. He also

side. Fool. That was poor Ben marked down as that most valuable of characters, as one who could play anywhere. Goodbye favoured position. Clarke of course said he was happy to oblige. 'If it means playing for England, I'll play anywhere,' he said in his customary affable, cheery, helpful way.

But England did have a dilemma. They wanted to play a wider game with a view to operating on the hard grounds of South Africa in the World Cup. Ideally they would slot a genuine number 7 in the Peter Winterbottom mould into the openside as a link man. Continuity would be the key. The problem was that the three best opensides in club rugby were Neil Back of Leicester, Andy Robinson of Bath and Derek Eves of Bristol. So what was the problem? About six inches . . .

The three are all under six foot tall. The case against the little men has intensified in the last couple of seasons simply because the laws have changed. With the ruling amended to that where the ball is turned over to the other side if it is not recycled by the attacking side at a maul, there is no longer the shrieking imperative for the attack-

The power play: Tim Rodber, thrusting through the tackles of Philippe Sellu and Guy Accoceberry, was at the forefront of England's driving play round the fringes of ruck and maul.

wondered whether he had made the right selection in two crucial positions – numbers 7 and 9. It was not as if Steve Ojomoh and Dewi Morris had been obviously lacking. Far from it. The game was so loose and one-sided that no England player was put under pressure. But Rowell always wants that little bit extra, that edge which divides winners from good performers. For Canada in December he went for Richards and Bracken, moving Clarke over to openside flanker.

The backrow, of historic wins over New Zealand and South Africa of recent history, was therefore reunited. It's a trio from hell, in bulk and performance one to strike terror into the hearts of every diminutive scrum-half or fly-half who has ever stood in their way. But one of the beauties of the sport is that being a bouncer in a rugby shirt is not enough. To be fair to the three

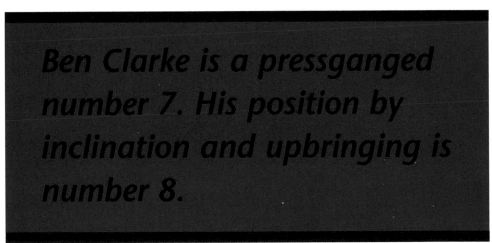

Ben Clarke is a pressganged number 7. His position by inclination and upbringing is number 8.

in question, they offered far, far more than meat and inches. However, they were not a classically formed backrow unit, and there was legitimate debate as to their effectiveness, perhaps even among themselves. 'It's an area of real concern for us,' said Les Cusworth.

Ben Clarke is a pressganged number 7. His position by inclination and upbringing is number 8. On the Lions tour to New Zealand in 1993 he stood in brilliantly at short notice on the open-

ing side to drive forward. In the old days the side who had forward momentum would get the ball. At a stroke the lawmakers altered one of the fundamentals of the game. Whatever the rights and wrongs of that particular discussion (and the wrongs far outweighed the rights) there was no disputing what its impact on the field was. As there was no longer the need to commit men to the maul so as to resist the forward drive, several forwards would therefore hang out on the

tors were entirely vindicated with all of them having outstanding seasons. For that, Tim Rodber, of all of them, would have breathed a huge sigh of relief. For just a few months earlier, on a dark, dark night in Port Elizabeth, it seemed as if his whole world was caving in.

Rodber was sitting on the bench that evening against Eastern Transvaal, presumably in a sound frame of mind. Three days earlier he had been the star turn in a star English performance in the first Test against South Africa. He had ridden tackles, punched holes, soared in line-outs and hit with the force of a demolition ball in the tackle. What he really needed then was a few days R and R and a gradual build-up to the second Test in Cape Town. Instead, as a stream of England players left the field injured by a bunch of madmen, Rodber found himself in the thick of a very unsavoury battle.

Now, acting army officers know all about coping with real bullets flying around him. But this was sport, and meant to be different. In a real battle keeping a level head must be a lot easier (mercifully few of us ever have to put our high falutin' theories to the test) whereas on a rugby field, there is only so much one can take. The point came when Rodber could take no more. A

edges and act as first-line tacklers. For an attacking side the need now was to find big men to knock these muggers out of the way. Cue the era of the massive backrow.

The argument is actually more complex than this. A player such as Back would argue, quite properly, that as continuity is now the key then the faster, smaller man is better equipped to get out wide and keep the game on the move. Back, whose fitness and ball-handling abilities, are on a plane beyond most other players in the world, finally did enough to convince the selectors of the merits of his case, and he was chosen, much to his own astonishment, for the World Cup squad. Both Geoff Cooke and then Jack Rowell had gone down the road of the giants, rendering the likes of Back an endangered species. 'English rugby went for the big men at the start of the year to provide us with space,' said Rowell. 'Neil Back gives us cover at openside and some added value in the game.'

If the discussion was sharp and involved at the time of the selection for the opening two matches against Romania and Canada, there was nonetheless little risk in opting eventually for the Rodber, Richards, Clarke line-up. Who could, or who would be brave enough, to take issue with these three? As it turned out the selec-

few minutes earlier he had seen full-back Jon Callard viciously stamped by Elandre van der Bergh. Half an inch further down and Callard would have lost his eye. Van der Bergh was merely spoken to by the referee. 'How much more do you have to do to get sent off?' Rodber asked the ref.

A few minutes later he found out. Another flare up and Rodber was in there trading punches. It was retaliation pure and simple. Rodber landed at least eight punches and was rightly sent off. He was only the second England player ever to be dismissed. Ironically the previous one, Mike Burton, was in the stands watching. Rodber was exonerated by the disciplinary panel and allowed to play in the second Test. Rodber though had another panel to face – his commanding officers back home.

In the furious aftermath of that disgraceful night, the one man who acted in exemplary fashion was Rodber. He knew what he had done was wrong, no matter the provocation. He was but a pale shadow of himself the following Saturday in the second Test, suggesting that it might have been better to have let him serve a suspension. It was perhaps Rodber's willingness to take his punishment on the chin which spared him a more serious grilling and reaction when he returned to his regiment, the Green Howards. 'Quite rightly I was made aware of my responsibilities as an army officer,' said Rodber later. 'It should not have happened.'

Rodber, 25 and a lieutenant, is a career soldier. He has been sponsored by the Army for almost ten years; as a 16-year-old at Churchers School in Hampshire, through Oxford Polytechnic where he read Human Biology and from there into active service. Twelve months ago he was allowed to step back from front line duties in order to concentrate on his rugby. He was assigned to the King's Division recruiting team where his time and movements are far more flexible. However, his time runs out at the end of the World Cup. Decisions then as to what he does will have to be made. 'It's reappraisal time,' says Rodber. 'Rugby has come first this season but the Army has always been my career. I'll have to evaluate just where I am. It won't be a snap decision. I'll have to weigh up many things.'

The arrangement has enabled Rodber to train far more assiduously and methodically. The benefits are obvious. He is a different, vastly improved player, central to England's success this season. Rodber, at 18 stone, is almost two stones heavier than he was in 1993. His training schedule, overseen by Northampton physio Phil Pask has had a complete overhaul. 'The quality and intensity of my work has improved,' says Rodber. 'What you need in rugby is time to rest as much as to train. I've got that at the moment. The result is that I'm fresher and fitter.'

And doesn't it show? He was to the fore in

Winging their way to success: The new adventurous approach brought England's wings into the game far more often, which was good news here for Tony Underwood and bad news for Ieuan Evans.

Attack, attack, attack: Guscott launches yet another England offensive as the Romanians scramble back to defend during their 54–3 defeat at Twickenham in November.

all the action at Lansdowne Road in January. England were favourites for the championship, which was just the sort of tag the Irish love ripping into. It had happened two years before when England came to Dublin a ludicrous 6-1 on to win. Ireland took them to pieces. Here, within about ten minutes of the kick-off, Rodber and his mates had completely neutered the Irish threat. The control and sense of conviction of England, in very difficult conditions with the winds howling, was reminiscent of the way in which they had flattened South Africa's hopes in the first Test. The style was different but the impact was the same. The match was as good as over after Carling's try. Rodber figured in that and was also a critical link in Tony Underwood's try in the second half. A 20-8 victory and England were on their way.

All they had to do now was beat the French, who had just won a series in New Zealand, a feat which had been beyond the whole of the British Isles a year earlier, then travel to Cardiff where they still only had one victory to their credit in over thirty years. Then they could put

their feet up and rest, assured that the Grand Slam was theirs because it was only the Scots coming to Twickenham for the final game and they would have lost all their matches by then. As we've said before, so unruffled and obvious does England's approach to the World Cup seem now, it's worth reminding ourselves at different stages just what the potential of the obstacles in their way actually was.

France were a dangerous proposition. Again England made the opposition look ordinary. This was not because they were ordinary, just that England made them look that way. Apart from a glitch in the line-out. England dominated up front. The BIG THREE won the backrow showdown against the vaunted French trio of Benazzi, Benetton and Cabannes with ease. Three more tries scored (one from Guscott and two by Tony Underwood) and England had chalked up their biggest win, 31-10, over France since 1911. Even so there was caution rather than euphoria in the air. 'England still have a lot of work to do when you see the southern hemisphere sides play,' said Rowell afterwards, a view echoed by his captain.

'We are getting fairly critical of ourselves,' said Carling. 'We have got to improve.'

In fact, England didn't improve, and yet they still won convincingly enough on the scoreboard, 23-9, in Cardiff. Rory Underwood's second try on the stroke of full-time saw England finish with a flourish but for much of the match they did not hit their customary fluent rhythm either up front or behind. Bracken and Andrew had trouble finding each other at half-back and the forwards had a battle in the set pieces up front. (Or they did until Welsh prop John Davies was sent off for supposed stamping after 62 minutes.) But what the hell. Another big win, and in Cardiff to boot. It's a mark of this England side that in the aftermath of victory they begin to sound more and more like All Blacks.

I'll never forget that great man of New Zealand Buck Shelford coming into the press conference after the All Blacks had put over fifty points on Wales (it was a rare occurrence in those days) and talking of the urgent need for his side to improve. Shelford was right. Self-criticism is not just the way to the top; it's the way to stay at the top. England have taken that on board this season, an attitude hardened by the arrival of Jack Rowell. Bath were always the same. They wanted, and never gave up searching for, that little bit more. Even if they hadn't needed it on that particular day, they knew that the day would come when they did need it. Extra time against Harlequins in the 1992 Cup Final. Who wins with the last kick of the match, a drop goal from 40 metres off virtually the only clean line-out they've won all afternoon? Bath. England were moving that way. So if the World Cup final goes to extra time and there's a line-out 40 metres from goal and . . .

Why should they have all the fun? Victor Ubogu breaks away from the traditional chores of a prop to join in the running extravaganza against Canada who succumbed 60–19 in December.

the World Cup

The world at their feet: Three members of the England squad – Graham Dawe, Jon Callard and Phil de Glanville, wonder if England will enjoy such a lofty position at the end of the World Cup.

So, right back to where they started from. Skies cloudless, seas inviting, surf invigorating, long, sandy beaches uncrowded – early winter in Durban. England will have no sleepy dust in their eyes this time round, no delusions about what lies before them and certainly no mixed feelings about being there at the end of a long season.

Last year the tour was important, but it was still just another tour. This time round it is the World Cup which would whet the appetite and stoke the competitive fears even if it were held in a railway siding at Crewe. Several players have had their sights on these four weeks ever since Derek Bevan blew his whistle to signal the end of the 1991 final against Australia. Deep down the likes of Brian Moore and Will Carling knew that England had not really done themselves justice that afternoon, that perhaps they were content just to be in the final and to acquit themselves well. Now there is a harder edge to their ambitions, a positive, wholly acceptable, sense of arrogance about their aims. To lose at any stage will be a catastrophic blow to their ego, and quite right, for there is no doubt that they have the potential to be World Champions. The problem is, so do four other sides. If they are to lift the Webb Ellis Trophy ('Old Bill' as the Aussies call it) on 24 June, England will meet at least three of them. If England emerge victorious they will have fully merited it for they have a tough old draw to negotiate. There is nothing too problematic in their group to worry about. Western Samoa are not the thunderous threat they were in 1991, having lost by over 70 points to Australia last summer, although the hard grounds and benign conditions will suit their style of play. Argentina have some ruffians up front to get the better of and a bit of pace behind, but again England should cope, even if they will remind themselves that Argentina beat Scotland twice barely a year ago. Italy have held their position since the last World Cup, which is more, sadly, than can be said of the likes of Canada and Romania. Italy

pushed Australia all the way last year in Brisbane, only going down in the final minutes by 17-13. Since then though they looked a little leaden and limited in losing to Wales in a World Cup qualifier. Three matches, three wins for England? It ought to be the case.

England's real World Cup could last all of 80 minutes. There is no doubt that they will go into their quarter-final as narrow underdogs, no matter who they face. While at one time the fourth group in the World Cup looked to be aptly named as the 'Group of Death' the subsequent performances of Canada and Romania have shown that label to be a few years out of date. England's opponents in the quarter-final in Cape Town will be either South Africa or Australia, effectively whichever loses the opening group match between the two of them.

All or nothing in the quarter-final then, which is of course how it should be in sport. The final four foot putt for the Ryder Cup, the 10 second 100 metre dash after four years of training, the long-range penalty attempt which drifts agonisingly wide in the last few seconds and England are out of the World Cup . . .

If it happens it will not be for want of trying or of preparation. This is the fittest, biggest, strongest, most thoroughly conditioned squad, in body, head and soul, to have ever left these shores. Each night the 26 players have ticked off the days on their fitness wall charts, scarcely being able to believe that tomorrow they had to get back out there and do it all again. They have pummelled bags, pumped iron, stretched and strained, all to be at a peak for these four weeks.

The physical size of the forwards is daunting. In fact they are probably the biggest group ever to be selected for England, a fact no better illustrated than in the surprise inclusion of Gloucester's Richard West as the reserve lock-forward. West, 24, with only one game for England A under his belt, got the nod over that veteran, loyal, proven campaigner Nigel Redman. Why? Simple really. West, 6ft 9in and 20 stone, has five inches and a few stones advantage over Redman. The Bath man was none too happy. 'Jack told me they'd gone for the bigger man,' said Redman. 'You do all the work, make all the sacrifices and then you're told you're not going because of your size. If it's done on size

On the slide? Brian Moore silenced those doubters who thought he might have past his peak and will once more lead the England pack into action in South Africa.

(previous pages) Danger all around: Tony Underwood tackles South Africa's Andre Joubert, one of the many danger men England will have to stop if they are to win the World Cup.

(opposite) Problems for referees? Lifting in the line-out, as Olivier Roumat soars so high for France, here with help from his friends, that he's in danger of needing oxygen.

what have I been doing with myself for the last year?'

More than any other selection Redman's omission shows just how hard-headed England are about their tilt for honours. No one would have batted an eyelid if Redman had been in the squad. But Rowell, who coached Redman at Bath for over ten years, thought that West could give him something extra. No other pundit in the country did, but Rowell did. There is no room for sentiment in this game.

As the players chase the game with seemingly nonchalant ease it's easy to overlook just how many buckets of sweat have been filled to get them to that state. They look supremely fit because they are supremely fit. They are driven

90

Violence: The sight of Jon Callard leaving the field with his eyebrow sliced open last summer in South Africa should serve as a sharp reminder for the need for self-discipline if the World Cup is to be a success.

by the desire to excel, to pit themselves against the best and to prove that they themselves are the best. Such are the thoughts that sustain them through the long hours of toil. Giving your all in front of 60,000 is a relatively easy matter. Putting your heart and lungs into training on a wet, cold night, so as to ensure that you will be in a position to give your all at Twickenham, is quite another matter. You had to feel for Redman when he said what he did. His pain will tell you all you need to know about how much these guys put in.

There was another who will have shared Redman's sense of injustice, although he refused

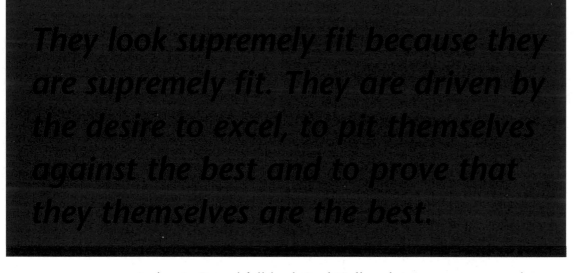

They look supremely fit because they are supremely fit. They are driven by the desire to excel, to pit themselves against the best and to prove that they themselves are the best.

to articulate it. Bristol full-back Paul Hull took it on the chin, merely saying that he would get on with life. He must have been lying, surely? In the quiet of his bedroom he must have wept. Twelve months ago in South Africa, Hull was the outstanding player in the England squad, the only one in those jaded, jittery opening weeks to play with any vigour and imagination. He was a revelation to us all. And then the gods decided to give him a good kicking. He was injured against Canada, Mike Catt came off the bench and the rest is history.

(following pages) To be repeated? England soak up the joy of success in South Africa after the frst Test. A repeat showing this summer?

Aside from Redman, and possibly Hunter over Hull, there can be no quibbling about the squad. It has a calm, settled air about it, and deservedly so. The hard work continues, with the squad meeting twice monthly again before departure. It seems to me as if they might benefit more by being packed off to Majorca for a week

to lie on the beach but as they've got everything right so far this season, then who am I to quibble. It's always a touch invidious to compare sides from different eras but this class of '95 seem to have their sights more firmly set than four years ago, and have a few more tricks up their sleeves too. They'll certainly need them.

'Perhaps we are no better in terms of individual capabilities than four years ago,' says Rowell. 'But we have taken a major stride forward in how to play the game. There is need still for more dynamism and flexibility and there is scope for spreading the ball wider and more systematically. But that's what we have been working hard on all season and will continue to do so.'

The squad will by now have done enough push-ups and shuttle runs to see them through the rest of their careers. What they will work on in the next few weeks are those few inches of sporting terrain which every champion has to conquer – the five inches between the ears. If their mind is not fully tuned in to the challenge then they will get some way but not all the way. 'The southern hemisphere teams have another dimension at the moment in terms of their mental preparation,' says Rowell.

The great David Campese who has been there, done that, scaled the heights, fallen off, clambered back up is actually training harder than ever at the moment. He is putting in three hours a day back in Sydney. In New Zealand Brian Moore's gnarled old adversary Sean Fitzpatrick has recorded better times at fitness camps than any of the youngsters in the squad. François Pienaar, the Springbok captain, says: 'The World Cup is the most important event in our lives. I know our players will be willing to pay whatever price is asked.'

All over the world the temperature is rising. Here, too, Carling's Men are steeling themselves to step into the furnace.

England
1994–5 results

54	England	Romania	3
60	England	Canada	19
8	Ireland	England	20
31	England	France	10
9	Wales	England	23
24	England	Scotland	12

Five Nations Championship

	P	W	D	L	F	A	Pts
England	4	4	0	0	98	39	8
Scotland	4	3	0	1	87	71	6
France	4	2	0	2	77	70	4
Ireland	4	1	0	3	44	83	2
Wales	4	0	0	4	43	86	0